The Modern Day Store

Becoming a Unified Store

The Modern Day Store

Becoming a Unified Store

Brian Barfield

**BUSINESS
BOOKS**

Winchester, UK
Washington, USA

First published by Business Books, 2012
Business Books is an imprint of John Hunt Publishing Ltd., Laurel House, Station Approach,
Alresford, Hants, SO24 9JH, UK
office1@jhpbooks.net
www.johnhuntpublishing.com

For distributor details and how to order please visit the 'Ordering' section on our website.

Text copyright: Brian Barfield 2012

ISBN: 978 1 78099 743 8

All rights reserved. Except for brief quotations in critical articles or reviews, no part of this
book may be reproduced in any manner without prior written permission from the publishers.

The rights of Brian Barfield as author have been asserted in accordance with the Copyright,
Designs and Patents Act 1988.

A CIP catalogue record for this book is available from the British Library.

Design: Stuart Davies

Printed and bound by CPI Group (UK) Ltd, Croydon, CR0 4YY

We operate a distinctive and ethical publishing philosophy in all
areas of our business, from our global network of authors to
production and worldwide distribution.

CONTENTS

Introduction

Many of you may have enjoyed the benefits of my first book titled *Modern Day Selling*. It was designed to help sales associates unlock their hidden potential and reconnect with their customers. As the world had evolved the styles and concepts of sales training were unable to keep up with such a changing environment. Thus we entered the era of greed, manipulation and bad sales tactics to try and gain an advantage over our customers and our competition. This has lead to a generation of sales associates who are leading unfulfilling sales career and are struggling to find lasting success. By exposing this great error in judgment with the truth, sales associates were given the keys to unlock their hidden potential. It was now time for the Modern Day sales professional to be born.

Through the many blessings that I have received from *Modern Day Selling* I have been able to become more connected with the retail sales community. No longer was my message being catered solely towards the jewelry industry. The retail industry as a whole embraced the truths that were discovered in *Modern Day Selling*. As avenues began to open throughout the retail world, my message began to really connect with people. These avenues lead to many opportunities to visit stores and impact their environments in a meaningful way. It was through these visits that I was able to see a pattern of need and desperation. There was something else that was hindering these stores from finding greatness.

It became very clear and evident that many of the stores in the retail world today had become disconnected. Through many years of neglect, the bond of trust and communication between owners and sales associates had slowly disappeared. There was now a great divide between the two and nobody knew how to reconnect. In a sense, it was like a modern day civil war was taking place within these stores. Somehow they had forgotten that they were once a team and a family. With this great disconnect arose many confrontations, hurt feelings and bitterness. Most of the power remained on the side of the owners, but without their sales associates on board they were powerless to grow and flourish. So, sales staff came, and went, but nothing really changed. There was always conflict, stress and disconnection. Something had to change!

This is how the birth of *The Modern Day Store* came to life. Having spent 18 years in the retail industry I had seen both sides of the fences equally. I had nine years experience as a head manager and nine years experience as an elite sale professional. I know the issues that both sides hold against each other. I have felt the power struggles that take place within our stores and the feelings of bitterness and un-appreciation. Therefore, I feel that it is my calling, and duty, to expose the chaos within our stores and bring to light the truth again to help lead the way to newfound freedoms as a unified team.

Owners, throughout this book you will find many great truths that will lead you to reconnecting your store and impacting its environment in a powerful way. No longer must you suffer through years of strife, conflict and disconnection. Today is your defining moment that will awaken within you a righteous fire to take back what has been stolen from you. Your store was not created or designed to live in defeat, suppression and division. You created your store with a vision of success, harmony and greatness in mind. It is my honor to share with you some fresh insight into where we went wrong and show you precisely how to fix it. With your leadership leading the way, and these great truths, you will be given the keys to unlock many treasures that have been hidden from you for far too long.

Sales associates, through this book you will find many great truths that will liberate you from your oppression and self-defeat. You have a purpose and meaning within your store to be a difference maker. No longer must you feel insignificant, powerless or defeated. Today is your defining moment that will awaken within you a righteous fire to claim what was once yours. You were hired to bring passion and energy to the store and be successful while impacting your customers' lives in a meaningful way. *Modern Day Selling* was your road map to help you find new lasting success with your customers. Now it is your turn to do your part and help unify your store. Once you achieve this, nothing can stop you from living your dreams and fulfilling your every desire.

Once a store becomes united it will find unlimited new successes together. The benefits of creating a unified store will be unending. Having been reconnected it will then be time to move forth together as a team and tackle many of the real issues that plague our stores today. It is here that you will be given a clear road map that will lead you to your destination of creating the Modern Day Store. Your environment will soon become a beacon of light that will draw in customers from far away. Your store will become a refuge from this crazy world where people will flock to feel the atmosphere that you have created. Your store will then give life and truth back to the world.

Finally, you will be given fresh insight on how to maintain this blessed environment. Once you have achieved this newfound success there will be a time of testing that you must be prepared for. The unrelenting enemies that used to operate within your store will always try to find their way back in using deception and disruptions. I will show you exactly what to watch for and how to overcome and endure your time of testing. You and your staff will now become warriors with the latest technology and weaponry to defend yourselves and your store environment. Never again will your stores have to suffer or be divided for you will hold the truths that shield you.

If you are tired of fighting the same old battles over and over I encourage you to open your heart and mind to the insight that you will be receiving this day. Whether you are an owner or a sales associate who has lost their way, this is the answer to your many years of prayers. All the meaningless years of turmoil will be exposed and you will be shown a clear path to exit your misery. Not only will my message impact your store but it will impact your life in a way that will bring about true and lasting change.

Chapter 1

The Great Disconnect

In the beginning you and your store were in unity. Before all the trials of business life there was a time when there was peace and unity. If you are an owner, you may be thinking back to the creation of your store as you and your very first staff set off on a journey into the unknown. There was a united passion set in motion by your leadership that defined the course of the beginning years. Can you remember those days when you and your staff were connected as one? You were ready to take on the world! What an exciting adventure it was! Then something happened along the way without you really noticing. You don't know when it happened, or how it happened, but something changed. Somewhere along the way there was a great disconnect that separated you from your staff, and things have never been the same.

If you are a sales associate, take a moment and remember back to the beginning of your sales career. Do you remember the undivided loyalty that existed between you and ownership? You would have marched to any order given with great pride as you followed your new leader. There was a fire and passion that was ignited within that made you feel invincible. Nothing seemed as if it could separate you and your destiny of success. Fast-forward to your current situation and what do you see? Better yet how do you feel about those who are in charge? What happened? Somewhere along the way there was a great disconnect that led you to your current situation.

As you read those first two paragraphs I bet many of you reflected of fond memories in the beginning. When those memories are awakened it creates a stirring within to get back to the good ole days. How we all long to find that passion and fire of so long ago. As a store owner you may have increased your business exponentially over the years, yet something is currently missing. Despite your growth in business you do not feel very successful as the grind of daily business has taken its toll on you. Something seems to be missing that you had once felt so long ago. You now feel more disconnected than ever and find yourself looking endlessly for the answers. Today, I am here to give you new insight that will revolutionize your store and its environment.

Now a question to the sales associates who read the first two paragraphs. What went through your mind during those moments of awakening? Doesn't something seem to be missing from your sales career? Even if you have sold millions of dollars in sales you may have never felt a sense of true accomplishment. In fact, many of you may feel very underappreciated and insignificant. Seasons come, and they go, but nothing really changes for the better. You may win a battle here and there, but you certainly feel like you are losing the war. The sales floor has become a grind that has taking its toll on your happiness. Selling no longer is a joy, but rather a way of making a living. If this is you, then today is a special day for you. The answers to your prayers have found you.

At this point you may be asking yourself, "Who is this guy and how does he know me so well?" To all of you I will answer that I am simply one of you. Through my 18 years in the world of retail I have experienced both sides of the fence equally. As a store manager of nine years I have felt the pressures and demands that weigh so heavily upon you owners and store managers. As a sales associate of nine years I have witnessed the passion come and go that is vital to bringing about success. I can truly say that I have felt your pain and longing for answers.

It was during the production of my first book, *Modern Day Selling,* that events unfolded which opened my eyes to see an epidemic that has swept through the world of retail stores. I experienced the decline and slow death of a positive store environment. It was through this experience that I witnessed a great divide that took place between ownership and the sales staff. What was once a great team suddenly became divided! It was so easy for each side to sit back and point the finger at whose fault it was. Both sides could make a great case before any judge. Through all the chaos was a store struggling for survival and needing a divine intervention.

Before I share my personal experience in such an environment let me share with you the history of this store. The store had grown strong over the years from a tiny little hole in the wall into an empire that set the standard for greatness in the local community. Obviously, the owners knew what they were doing and provided a great environment for sales associates to find big time success. By the time I had arrived it was a $3,000,000 powerhouse leaving every other local jewelry store behind in the dust. It was anchored by two strong sales associates who had been with them for quite some time. One of them was a $1,000,000 sales associate who had a following that was very loyal and dedicated to her.

When I arrived it was a well-oiled machine that needed very little maintenance to operate. The amount of experience and expertise that existed made it a professional environment that was geared for success. Clearly the owners had done many things right and hired very well. A majority of the sales staff were ex-store managers who knew how to manage themselves, therefore making the owners' and managers' jobs much easier. Things were really rolling in the right direction. After a few years as a sales associate I had built up a large and loyal customer base using the skills that I shared with you in *Modern Day Selling*. I had quickly found my way to the top of the sales charts while maintaining a great working relationship with the staff. My addition to the team and a beautiful new store location had taken the store from $3,000,000 to $4,500,000 all during the tough economic times that our nation was experiencing.

Through all our success there were occasionally minor disagreements that we always quickly soothed over in order to maintain such a successful work environment. Overall, there was a good understanding and communication between sales associate and ownership. We had found great success by following the golden rule that if it isn't broken don't try and fix it. Then slowly something began to change. One of the owner became unsatisfied with the success that we had achieved and begin to focus obsessively on little negative things that were very insignificant. Slowly this constant negativity began to impact the store's environment in a negative way and eventually created a separation between ownership and sales associates. Over the next few months the store continued to find success based on the solid foundation that was laid over the years, but working there was not the same. Everyone began to dislike their jobs and we constantly found ourselves looking for 6 pm to arrive daily. When Saturday arrived we were all relieved to make it through another week. Everyone began to live for the weekends.

We were no longer a team united anymore. The store had become completely divided with ownership on one side and sales associates on the other. Stuck in the middle was a store manager who hated his job and agreed with both sides far too often. Over that year every new sales associate besides me and the two core sales associates had left. There became a constant state of turnover throughout the store and it was only a matter of time before something would happen that would push us all to the point of no return. That time was just around the corner.

It was just before the Christmas season of 2011 that a chain of events occurred which would forever change the store and its environment. Over the previous years the owner had become increasingly unhappy within. He was very critical and unappreciative of the people who were working hard to make him successful. He began to speak to everyone who would listen of his displeasure with everyone and everything within the store. Some he singled out more than others. It was the office manager and store manager that took the brunt of the blows and insults. As he became more increasingly unhappy he began to make decisions out of desperation that impacted the store in a very negative way.

It was November of 2011 that the beginning of the end began. The owner felt like there should be more money flowing in so he decided to implement a new policy. Without warning it was laid out to us that anyone who discounts more than 5% would have to split the sale with the store thus losing half of the sales commission. This did not sit well with any of the sales staff because we had worked so hard already to maintain certain profit levels. We prided ourselves on never discounting more than 10%. The store was financially secure because of the hard work we had done. So why was this happening?

It is greed that is often found somewhere in the equation when a store begins to become disconnected. Greed's main goal is to first sever the bond of trust and interrupt the lines of communication. It is here that a store becomes vulnerable and defenseless as greed begins to choke the life right out of the store environment. It was now very evident that greed had taken root within the store, and it was growing rapidly. This led to many moral issues in the store that Christmas. Every little thing that popped up was now intensified because the line of communication and bond of trust had been severed.

It just so happens that during this time a mistake was made on commissions that were already paid out a few months earlier. The company had overpaid us on three large sales that involved a trade-in. Without saying a word, the company had decided to take back the proper portion of commission that was overpaid to me and the other top sales associate within the store. With it being Christmas time I guess they thought we would not notice. They were actually justified in deducting the amount from the current month but the way they went about it was very inappropriate. All we knew is that few hundred dollars of commission had suddenly disappeared. These are the kind of things that will happen when the lines of communication have been broken.

Obviously this led to even more mistrust and bitter feelings within the store. Both sides dug in and began to strategize on ways of defeating one another. Through this strategizing process it was discovered that it was actually illegal to take back commission from employees who had already been paid. The owners had broken the law! What a powerful weapon this would be to blow through their defenses! Guess what, they did not care. In their minds it was the right thing to do and even I agreed that it was the right decision. Here it was Christmas time and we were all focused on issues that could have been handled differently. What was normally a small molehill was being turned into a mountain. Greed had done its job very well.

At this point there were feelings of hurt and bitterness evident on both sides. Because of the previous policy change, we sales associates felt as if we were being squeezed for every nickel by our cheapskate owners. It appeared as if they were pinching every penny and trying to make the store more profitable at any expense. It was the way that they were implementing their decisions that was totally leading us into a confrontation of epic proportions. Everyone was left feeling unappreciated and cheated. What followed was a chain of events that led to them almost losing everything.

After Christmas I looked back at the amount of sales that I intentionally allowed to walk because I refused to split the sale with the company. There were about five sure sales that could have given us another $25,000 to the month. Because I was confident in my abilities I was willing to make a statement and stand up for those who were weaker and needed the money. In this case it was more about character and respect than money. The weird thing was that we had just experienced the most profitable Christmas in company history. Things seemed to be OK from the owners' perspective, but there would be a big price to pay forthcoming with long-term negative effects. The damage had already been done.

Since the changes were made at Christmas time they did not feel the effects until afterwards. The following three months we missed our goals by very large amounts. It would have been four months in a row had I not closed sales of $27,000 and $37,000 the last few days of that month. After a brief moral victory we proceeded to drop the next month by $100,000. The store was now in a free fall. In March the office manager of six years who was the eyes and ears of the store left because of the years of abuse and lack of appreciation. The following month the old store manager resigned, leaving us very shorthanded. Those who were already planning their exit strategies were beginning to pick up the pace as the ship was clearly sinking faster than anticipated.

As I look back I can see with clarity that there were things that we as sales associates could have done to help out the owner. He was really not a bad guy. He had just lost his way through the struggles of business life and found himself far away from the success he once knew. Without being able to see things clearly he panicked and made some really bad decisions. We all have moments in our lives where we lose our way. We should have been there to support him and help guide him gently back to the path he had found so much success in following. Instead we were relentless in our efforts to show him something he was not willing to see. For every finger we pointed his way we should have been pointing one back towards ourselves. The bottom line was this was his store and he could do with it as he pleased.

Being a store manager for nine years, I should have recognized the enormous pressure that he was under. He must have felt like someone who was stranded on a deserted island just wanting to reconnect with society again. Many would say that he isolated himself and got what he deserved. However, I believe that we should have been there for him and helped him a little more than we did. If a member of your family is struggling many of us will do everything within our power to help them out. Even if you can't rectify the situation you still consider them as part of the family. You do not disown them and leave them alienated. I will share with you an instance where we as sales associates could have done things differently.

These are the kind of things that will take place on both sides when you have a divided store. It was a showdown between the owner and myself. One of my best clients had previously received a discount before the policy changed at our diamond sale event. When they came back to exchange it after Christmas I was told that the new sale would have to be split with the house if I gave the same discount. Everyone looking from the outside in was in disbelief, especially my loyal customer who has spent a lot of money with us. So I told the customer what the new policy was and that the 15% off they received at the special event would now only be 5% due to this policy change. They were in shock! I apologized and told them that if I owned the store that I would do things differently, but a decision had been made that I could not change.

She then told me how much she appreciated me and that I was the only reason that they shopped at the store. She went on to explain that they had a bad experience a few years before I arrived and that she could not believe that her husband, a well-known doctor, had decided to do business with us again. I gave her hug and thanked her for her support. She left with no bag in hand that day. Later I did do the right thing and gave her the discount and split it with the store. I had realized that one of my favorite customers should not have to pay the price of a horrible business decision. I allowed my frustration to impact the customer's life in a negative way which was totally incorrect.

Afterwards I was so proud of myself for standing up to such

injustice. I thought that I had just taught the owners a very valuable lesson. Maybe they would see the errors of their ways? The fact of the matter is that they simply did not care. Losing a few clients was worth it to them in order to bring about the change they wanted. I should not have brought the customer into the situation with me. My job was to give the customer an amazing experience and I should have put their needs above my own. I should have just split it with the house and swallowed the bitter pill. Even if this policy change took away my well-deserved income, it was not worth risking my entire job over. Now, I was contributing negatively to the situation just as much as the owner was.

The previous true story is the perfect illustration on how a store can become disconnected very quickly. Anyone looking from the outside in could clearly see that things were handled improperly on both sides and could have been handled better with the appropriate communication. This is the kind of struggle that often happens around the country. These types of situations can divide a store for good and force many good sales associates to leave and walk away. In our case it did just that.

Because our situation was so severe and created such a disconnection, almost every single employee began to plan an exit strategy. Some left quickly within the first few months and others lined up future endeavors before leaving the company. I was just one of the many who had enough. Some of us stayed for a while, but in reality they lost everyone that Christmas and it was only a matter of time before they paid the consequences of their actions. What a sad sight it was to witness such division within the store. The once unified store that achieved greatness together and climbed to new heights had suddenly begun to free fall.

The fact is that anyone could take a side and make a strong case as to who was in the wrong. The bottom line is that we were both in the wrong and could have done many things differently to keep the lines of communication open. To this day I look back upon what was once great and I am saddened to watch it crumbling from the inside out. I remember all the good times and how it used to be.

Now, our store was in the middle of a divorce and our relationship seemed to be irreconcilable. In a relationship people are able to make many mistakes and find forgiveness. However, there are certain actions that can take place which make things almost impossible to reunite the two as one again. The final big mistakes were made that Christmas which led to the ultimate disaster that took place over the next year. I have decided to use this horrible experience in the best way possible to expose our disconnections within our stores and bring about the unity that we once held so dear. It is time for owners and sales associates across the country to reunite and rekindle the flames of unity that that they once used to have so long ago.

I feel that it is my duty and calling to bring about change in the world of retail sales. It is through my unique experience of finding understanding on both sides of the fence that I have gained the insight and vision necessary to lead you to becoming a unified store once again. In order to start such a journey we must first start at the root of the problem and expose the issues that bring division upon us. What better way to do this than to look at life experiences and translate them over into the world of retail sales.

Many of us have had the experience of being united in marriage at some point in our lives. You remember the beginning of your relationship with fond memories of passion and desire. The first months of any relationship are exciting, liberating and joyous. At that time you felt invincible and that nothing could separate the love you shared together. It was this confidence that led you to the altar to be united together in marriage. What a wonderful defining moment it was in many of our lives. Things would never be the same.

It is this same scenario that takes place the moment that an owner finds a sales associate to unite with on a journey together towards greatness. Both have visions of a lifetime of success together as they conquer the world of retail together. Owners, take a moment and think back to when you hired your current sales staff. There was something that you saw within each sales associate that could benefit you and your store. At that very moment they had a value and a purpose to help you find success. You were thrilled to have them on your staff and saw a bright future ahead. Nothing was going to separate you and your new sales associate from finding success together.

Sales associates, take a moment and think back to the moment that you were hired. The fact that you applied and accepted a job tells me that there was something that you loved about your company. You felt accepted, needed and valuable. You decided at that very moment that you were going to work hard for your boss and be a dedicated sales associate because they saw something special in you. Nothing was going to separate you and your owner from finding success together.

Just like marriage, the moment you hired or were hired a vow was made to unite the two together and become one. Owner and sales associate were meant to find a lifetime of happiness together. I think we all could agree that the beginning our relationship together had special moments full of excitement and great expectations. I will ask you now to come back to the present and examine your relationship with your sales associate or owner. What do you see now? Has anything changed? What were your first thoughts when you examined your feelings of that owner or sales associate? I am pretty sure that they were not the thoughts that you were thinking moments ago. What happened?

I can tell you exactly what happened! Through all the craziness of life and business you simply drifted apart. What was once a thriving and stable relationship full of potential has slowly dissipated away leaving you sad, lost and looking for answers. Just like a marriage relationship, the realities of business life roll over us like a wave with unrelenting force, pushing us further and further away from one another. As I share this I am sure many of you are feeling a stirring within to try and make things right again. It is my hope and prayer that you owners and sales associates come to such an awakening at this very moment and realize just how far you have drifted away from one another. The fact that you have read thus far tells me that you want to make it right again. Both of you desire to rekindle that flame of passion and desire that was evident when you first united together on your journey to success.

I am here to share with you that there is way back to finding peace and harmony. This book is a road map that will lead you out of the dark and back onto the path that leads you to a unified store. There is hope if you will open your heart and mind and take the necessary steps forward to reconnecting. With a little dedication and a lot of hard work you can become great once again.

In order to move forward we must first look back to examine where things went so wrong. When you are able to see your setbacks with clarity then an awakening takes place within and hope is born. The best way to do this is to continue to relate this situation to the example set to us by the experiences we see in marriage. After the wedding and honeymoon take place reality sets in and we realize that we are two very separate people. When you are around one another daily you begin to see the real individual that your spouse truly is. You see the good, the bad and the ugly. It is easy to love when all you see is good coming forth from those you love. What happens when the bad and ugly start to make their presence known? Doubt sets in and you begin to question whether or not you made the right choice.

This is the first stage of disconnection that takes place between owners and sales associates. Do you remember the first time your new sales associate did not met your expectations as quickly as you liked? How about the first time your owner displayed harsh or negative words towards you? You both thought, "This is not the person I thought they were? Maybe I made the wrong choice?" This, my friend, is your first enemy called doubt. It is doubt that takes root within your mind and begins to lead you away from the confidence you once held onto so dearly.

It is when this scenario take place repeatedly that you begin to lose focus on what is really important. Instead of focusing on growing together you begin to let doubt set you back. You begin to focus solely on the negatives of that individual which lead you to a false reality. All the good that was once clearly seen has been overshadowed by the darkness of doubt. Suddenly you forgot what the one you cared about so dearly looked like. Their beauty has simply faded away. The ironic thing is that they are every bit as beautiful and full of potential as the day you connected together in unity. Nothing has really changed but your focus and perception. I hope it is evident that doubt leads you to enemy number two, which is false reality.

What happens next in the process of disconnecting from one another is good ole fashioned panic. Your false reality that you have created has now led you to a state of panic. What am I going to do? This is not what I signed up for. The owner begins to allow the seed of panic to grow and thinks, maybe I should fire them? The sales associate begins to allow the seed of panic grow and thinks, maybe I should quit? Now you have doubt, false reality and panic working together in unity which leads you to enemy number four which is chaos.

When the relationship between owner and sales associate reaches the level of chaos, it pushes many over the edge on a downward slope to anger and despair. Now the one you once thought of so fondly seem to have become your worst nightmare. There seems to be no more joy or fun left in the relationship at this point. It has become toilsome and more of a burden for you.

You begin to think to yourself, "Why should I have to put up with this? I was better off before all the troubles this person brought me. It is their entire fault!" Now you are totally disconnected and at your wits' end. It just seems easier to put each other out of their misery than to continue on such a course of destruction.

This is the way that we allow many of our stores to operate these days. Totally disconnected and divided. Sales associates come and go but nothing really changes. Both sides feel disrespected, underappreciated and hurt. It has left behind a path of destruction and chaos that could have been avoided if only we had the right answers. If only we had the proper insight to see things more clearly to intervene and act before these negative traits take root and destroy our stores and their environments. There has to be a better way to operate our business and find sanity. I am here as a messenger to answer such questions, give you newfound freedoms and create life again within your store. By the time you finish this book you will have the answers to help you reconnect and create a unified store.

Chapter 2

A Message to Owners

In this chapter I have a message for the owners of today's retail store. It is a message of understanding, clarity and insight. After reading chapter one I am pretty sure I connected with your thoughts and feelings on many occasions. It is you who have taken a seed of vision and planted it within your store in hopes that it will grow into something beautiful and prosperous. You have taken the time, care and energy needed to bring life to your store and its environment. Just as God created you in His own image, so you have now created your store in your own image. It is your creation and you have the power to do with it as you please.

With such power comes a great responsibility to grow and maintain your creation. There are so many things that must be done in order to grow your business into something beautiful. There are the basics of finding a good location and then building a beautiful store. Then you must find the right merchandise that appeal to your market. Now a sales staff is needed to give excellent service and provide a wonderful experience for your customers. Then you must advertise and find ways to create desire within your customers to shop with you at your store. The checklist is unending, as well as the pressures and demands it creates. The process is toilsome, yet rewarding, and here you are reading this book.

With me being the founder and creator of *Modern Day Selling* I understand you and your unique situation. I know the risk involved in venturing out into the unknown with a vision and a belief in what I am pursuing. It takes great faith and passion to take off on such a journey on your quest for success. At the time you did not know exactly what awaited you along the path you were taking. The truth is that everything was waiting for you along your path. There is a time and season for everything you encounter along the journey of your career. There is time to begin and a time to end; a time for success and a time for failure; a time for loving your career and time for hating your career; a time to grow and time to cut back. I could go on forever listing things that you have encountered or will encounter during your reign as king of the store.

Having a clear understanding of these seasons as they take place is very important in helping you grow and complete your store. I call these special moments that take place within your store defining moments. They are like pieces to a puzzle that help you create the full picture of your success. Until you are able to put the pieces together all you have is a defining moment with no vision of the big picture. However, when you are able to piece these moments together something magical takes place. It is the divine understanding of your purpose and meaning in your life as a retail store owner. With this knowledge you will be able to see with clarity the purpose and calling that you have to impact people's lives of many different ways.

So let's examine some possible defining moments that have taken place in your store thus far. Before we do this you must first ask yourself whether it was truly a defining moment or just a memory. Defining moments can easily be identified by the lasting impact it has had on your store, either good or bad. Memories quickly fade away and become just what they are, memories. In order to help you get a better understanding I will share with you a few scenarios of defining moments that could take place in a store environment.

A great example of a defining moment would be the moment you choose what type of store you would operate. Would it be a branded store with set prices or a non branded store where price was negotiable? Both options have their pros and cons. You could sit back and debate for an hour which is better. However, the choice that you made defined the way that you chose to conduct your business.

Another example of a defining moment is who you chose to manage your store. Would they be a motivator or a firm dictator? Again either option could be debated as to which is more beneficial. However, your choice defined the role of leadership within your store. That choice will also impact other things that are important to your success like your store environment. I think you see the theme here is that the choices you make define your store and its environment. Being an owner can be very difficult because the choices you make can often lead to lasting results that are good or bad.

The last defining moment that I will share with you is each and every sales associate that you hire. They are the DNA of your store and its environment. They can bring you much joy and success or much misery and heartache. This is an area that I will be more specific on later in this book. Why? Because how you view and treat your sales associates is a key ingredient to creating your current store's environment.

Now I want to take this concept of defining moments and ask you owners to do something personal with it. I would like for you to apply this concept to your life in general. In *Modern Day Selling* I called it the power of self-examination. Looking within the mirror of your soul to see the real you. Until you are able to see yourself more clearly then you will not be able to lead your store into the promise land that you so desire. Open your mind and look at who you have become. What do you see when you examine yourself and your life's history? What defining moments took place within your life that created the person you are today? Who exactly are you and what messages are you sending to your staff?

I will start by sharing with you a few defining moments that have taken place throughout my life. I would not ask you to do such an examination without giving you a few examples of things to explore. Please remember that for just this moment we are moving away from business and into your personal life. Here are a few examples of defining moments that have happened in my life that have had lasting impacts on me and my life. These defining moments range from insecurities created in childhood to defining moments of adulthood. Every one of them had a lasting effect on me no matter how small or great they appear to be.

My first defining moment that I can remember happened to me when I was four. It was the first time that I had a crush on a little girl in my preschool class. I did what any four year old would do. I sent my friend over with a message to profess my love for her. What happened next has stuck with me forever. The little girl and her friend began to laugh at me, and started throwing wooden square blocks as me. I quickly ran and took cover behind a large wheelbarrow as they hurled insults and blocks my way one after another. I will never forget the shame that I felt at that very moment which led to years of insecurity in my life. This was certainly a defining moment that took place within my life.

Growing up I have faced rejections from other people, but none of them had the lasting effect that this defining moment had in my life. The rest were just bad memories that quickly faded away. I wanted to share this defining moment with you to help you understand the difference between a defining moment and a memory. It is amazing how something so childish could have such a powerful effect on my life. Many insecure years later I was able to face this defining moment with truth and expose the lie that I had bought into. Seeing your life with clarity really helps you overcome these bad defining moments.

The next defining moment that I will share with you is good defining moment. It is one that many of you may have experienced yourself. It was the birth of my son Austen. For that one special moment in time when I held him in my arms for the first time, life had a newfound purpose and meaning. In an instant my life was changed for the better and I knew that a defining moment had just taken place. Years later I still look back and remember every single detail of that moment. It was more than just a memory. It helped define who I am today in many different ways.

The final defining moment that I will share with you is one of great loss. We all must go through such experiences in life. It is simply unavoidable. My brother and his wife had been trying to have children for many years unsuccessfully. Finally the moment had arrived where they were blessed with triplets. In the beginning we were all a little worried about the triplets and my sister-in-law's safety. After six months a renewed spirit of excitement swept through the family as we awaited these three little blessings. Everything seemed to be so perfect, until the phone range one evening. She had gone into labor early and the triplets had a small chance of survival. However, they were all still alive and we viewed this as God setting the stage to do a great miracle.

Within two days they all had returned to their maker and we were left with many unanswered questions. What a devastating blow this was to our family. I have never cried so uncontrollably in all my life. At this very moment tears are forming as I share this defining moment with you. What happened that evening would change my life forever. Life now had a more special meaning to me. My heart began a transformation that night that is still taking place to this very day. Somehow I have slowly become a better person through such tragedy. Always remember that through tragedy some of life's greatest transformations can begin to take place. The choice of whether it is good change or bad change is solely up to the individual to decide.

So, now I ask you to examine such moments that have happened in your life. Look upon these moments with truth and bring them to light. Explore the impact that these defining moments had in your life. How has it affected you and your ability to lead your people within your store? I am sure you will find a few defining moments that have created wonderful characteristics within you which have helped you lead your stores and impact the environment in a powerful way. Those are always fun to examine and look upon with pride.

It is even more important to take a look at the defining moments that have created negative traits within you. It is these moments that you must focus intently on no matter how painful it may be. In these negative defining moments you will find some of the answers to the problems that take place within your store and its environment. Now, I am not saying that you are the main problem in your own store. You are the boss and have the right to do whatever you please. However, you are the leader of your store and lasting change starts with you. Sales associates should do the same self-examination process and do their part too. After all you are a team and everyone must do their part.

Sometimes owners forget that they must do their part in creating change in order to be truly successful. Because they hold such great power they sometimes feel as if they should just discard anyone who gets in their way or disagrees with them. That last statement is a very true statement; it also is a deadly statement. A thought process like that will only lead you in a vicious cycle of constant transition with very few positive results. Sales associates will come and go and your stress level will reach new heights as you lose your sanity. Always remember that vanity leads to insanity within a store.

As you look back over your life and see how things have affected you I encourage you to share this insight with someone who you trust. It could be your spouse, a fellow owner, or a close friend. Don't try to implement change within all by yourself. Those who know you best will make sure that you are heading in the right direction. Sometimes they see you more clearly than you see yourself. This process of personal growth will be liberating for both you and your store. This is the first step to unifying a store and its environment.

Many of you owners may be feeling a little under attack at this moment. It may be hard to swallow that you are the first main ingredient to creating a unified store. Why should you have to listen to this? You have the power to fire me at this point just like you do with your sales associates. This is a normal thought process when someone is exposed to truth that they do not want to hear. Yes, you do have the right to fire me right at this very moment, but I can assure that your store will never be unified or reach its full potential. My experiences in retail have shown this to be true time and time again. I ask you to hold tight because I will be dealing with the sales associates in the next chapter. Just like many sales associates reading this chapter are singing hallelujah brother, preach it, you will be doing the same in the next chapter. I promise! We all need to make change in order to be unified.

Chapter 3

A Message to Sales Associates

Sales associates, it is time to buckle up your seat belts! It is going to be an exhilarating yet bumpy ride. Before we go any further I want to share with you that I feel your pain. I know what it is like to feel underappreciated and powerless to do anything about it without receiving major ramifications. A majority of the first part of my career was spent more on the management side of things where I held a position of power over sales associates. However, I have spent the last seven years of my career as a sales associate and I have witnessed firsthand the injustice that appears to be taking place against you. Life as a sales associate is very difficult these days. I know each and every one of you wishes that your boss would do an undercover boss show and take over your job for a month. Then they might appreciate you a little more and see how valuable you really are.

However, I ask you to stop and think for a moment about your boss. Think of the enormous amount of pressure that they are under. If you were suddenly asked to take over their job for just one week you would have a newfound respect for them and their position. I promise you that many of you have absolutely no idea how tough the life of an owner can be. If you thought your job was difficult, try having to make tough decisions every day that affect everyone's life around you. It is impossible to make everyone happy. Just like this book is going to be impossible to make all of you happy.

Let me share with you that your owner probably cares for you more than you will ever know. Deep down inside they understand that you are the single most important thing to helping them find success. Without you, who would take care of the customers they worked so hard to bring into the store with advertising? You are the lifeblood that keeps a store running and operating. Sure they could replace you, but why would they want to do that? All the training and experience they would lose would set them back months or years. They may not admit it often, but trust me they care. As a manager for nine years I often found myself frustrated with my employees, but in the end I knew that without them I could not find the success I desired.

There is one thing that I need to make crystal clear to all sales associates. Many of you do not have a clue what is actually going on behind the scenes. That is exactly why you are sales associates. Every decision that is made is often done with careful thought, and has a plan to lead you to success behind it. You may not understand the reasons why a certain policy was changed, but I assure you that often there is a good reason. I have complained with the best of them. At times you think, "Have they lost their minds? What are they thinking? I don't agree with this." Some times you may actually be right. However, you should do exactly what you were doing and that is just thinking it.

Instead of just thinking about our strong opposition, what do many of us do? We express our displeasure with everyone else. We build a sales associate militia to form a resistance against such tyranny. You think, if we unite then they will see the error of their ways and change will come forth. The problem is that change that you desire will rarely ever come about. Many times you are left leading the charge only to find out that nobody is charging with you. They left the fight long ago. Even if such resistance holds tight, the odds of a positive outcome are definitely not in your favor. What are you doing? The best thing to do is keep your thoughts to yourself and quit tainting your environment with negative energy. Many times sales associates think that the owners are the main problem (maybe they are) when in fact you have now become an even bigger problem. This is no way to handle such a situation, yet we often find ourselves doing it over and over again.

In your disagreement with policy or decision making you forgot one important thing. That is that you are not in charge and this not your store. You did not invest millions of dollars and years of hard work to create a functioning retail store. The important calls are not yours to make. All you have become now is another form of cancer within the store and its environment. You are quickly on your way to being terminated. It is OK to privately express your opinion or concerns, but to drag everyone else into the situation is the wrong way of going about it. In this situation you are now viewed as the problem even if you have the right answers to the store's situation.

As I moved along further in my sales career I often found myself struggling to keep my mouth shut. Most of the time I did express my opinion behind closed doors and often they listened to me because they understood that I have a lot of insight into building a store and its environment. Then there were times where we did not see eye to eye, and it was my duty to follow along the path that was being laid before me. That is a very hard thing to do when you think you know a better way. However, I have learned over time that the owners often knew what they were doing and things almost always seem to turn out just fine.

We as sales associates have a great responsibility to do our part in creating a positive store environment. When we allow situations to interrupt the positive flow of energy we often find ourselves becoming bitter and disconnected. Just like the owners have a responsibility to communicate with us, we must do the same with the utmost respect. If you have ever noticed, it is generally the senior sales associates who often express their displeasure more frequently because they feel entitled. I know that when I began to become noticed around the country suddenly I started to feel entitled to say exactly what I thought and felt. I had to put the brakes on my ego and teach myself to be humble and respectful again.

To all you elite sales professionals out there, I ask you to examine your mindset towards your owners and how you treat them. If you see that you have become resistant, or defiant, I strongly recommend that you make the necessary changes to become a good team player again. This is a great pitfall that has ended the careers of many a great sales professional. Sure you could go find another location to sell, but there are negative impacts that will follow along with you. First, most of your clientele will not follow you. It could take years to establish yourself to the level of success you currently have. Secondly, you become labeled as a problem maker and word gets around the selling community quickly.

As sales associates we all have had our moments where we did not meet the high standards of professionalism that have been set over time. The best thing that you can do is learn from your mistakes and share it with others. There is no lasting shame in making a mistake. In fact, you can take your shortcomings and impact the sales world with your knowledge and wisdom that you have obtained. As I was writing this book I wavered on opening up and sharing some of the mistakes that I have made. I felt it might tarnish my image, or make me look weak. However, I have come to understand that people often respect you more when they are able to see that you are vulnerable and prone to make mistakes just like they are.

I want you as sales associates to understand that something powerful takes place when you expose your mistake or short-coming. When you shed light on your blunders the lasting negative effects are powerless to operate. Take a moment and think about that last statement. You make a mistake. You own up to your mistake. Then you share insight to help others around you in order to better your environment. This is a key to putting the handcuffs on negativity and bad energy. It is a great way for you to grow as a team and find a higher level of success together.

Exposing your mistakes can actually be a team-building experience.

Just about anything negative in your career as a sales associates can eventually be used for good if you choose to do so. I had a situation that occurred right before my new career path took off as a sales trainer and teacher. As I mentioned before our store was filled with negativity and was very disconnected. My manager came up to me and snapped at me about the description that I had written on a repair envelope. I looked it over with him and pointed out all the little things that I did correctly. I put the millimeter of every diamond followed by a very detailed description. My manager shot back at me that I did not mention that the girdle was thin to thick. I exploded back, "Have you lost your mind? Anyone here would look at that description and tell you it was perfectly OK." So we left it at that.

The next day we met privately and it came to light that the owner had forced him to write me up. I signed the write up and fired an angry e-mail to the owner expressing my displeasure. My words were along the lines of, "If you look at the repair ticket you will see that I did my job well and protected the company well. Is this how you treat your top performers? Do you greet those who make you money with a slap or a kiss? Anyone with common sense would tell you that you should greet them with a kiss." Every word I spoke was 100% truth. The other sales associates were so happy to hear someone finally speak up and tell it like it was. However, I later asked myself, "Was I being a good leader? Was I impacting the store environment in a positive way?" The answer was no and I had to learn from my mistake.

The odd thing was that at the next managers meeting the owner asked to see the repair ticket. After closely examining the invoice, it was determined that there was nothing wrong with the description that I had written. All this nonsense was over nothing! The fact was that the manager and I were very good friends. Something else was stressing him out and he later admitted that he took it out on me. These are the kind of encounters that happen when you have a divided store and a negative work environment. The next time something happens to you that does not make any sense, please take a brief moment and think things through with clarity. Make sure that you remain silent. If after a while you still feel strongly, ask to speak to them behind closed doors. I was written up for not filling out a ticket properly which was not the case. However, I should have been written up for disrespecting the manager in public.

At the beginning of this chapter I mentioned how I can relate to your issues with the way you are treated at times. After reading the story above I am sure many of you recalled times of injustice or feeling powerless to react. The fact of the matter is that those times are going to happen. Ownership and management are not perfect. It is when the store environment is tainted with negativity that these issues occur more frequently because of stress and frustrations building. In order to start making a change it is very important to step back and examine the ways that you contribute to your store's environment. We as sales associates have a duty to follow orders and the leadership set in place.

Being a sales associate in today's world can be very challenging and exhausting. I would like you all to remember just how important you are to your store's success. Just like an army is powerless to operate without its soldiers, your store is powerless to find success without you. With this knowledge comes a great responsibility to know and accept your role as a soldier of the store. When orders are given it is your responsibility to execute the plan set in motion and be victorious. Without your compliance and execution the chances of achieving victory are very slim.

I want you to take a moment and think about that last statement. What would have happened if soldiers refused to follow orders or execute the plan set forth by their superiors?

First, there would be no victory. Secondly, there would be negative consequences to follow if they survived. Could you imagine how D-Day would have turned out if the soldiers all disobeyed orders and left the fight? Those soldiers went into battle knowing that there would be a great sacrifice to pay and that many of them would pay the ultimate price. Still they followed orders and went forth into battle with the mindset that they were the liberators of the world. There was a purpose worth fighting for that was greater than themselves. They were willing to sacrifice it all for the greater good of freedom and victory.

If there is anything that you take away from this chapter I hope it is this one important fact. You are the liberators of your store and its environment. It is you who are on the front line facing many pressures and oppositions. As you overcome each obstacle you become more battle tested and skilled to bring about victory. Do not allow fear of the unknown to keep you from achieving your goal of victory. Follow the plan that is set in motion to bring about victory as a unified team. When you do this I assure you that victory is very imminent in your future. You may not win every battle but if you remain unified I assure you that you will win the war.

Chapter 4

The Great Awakening

So far we have discussed the great disconnection that has taken place within many of our stores today. Hopefully, you can see with more clarity that we have allowed our stores to become a battlefield. The sad truth is that nobody ever really wins. The owners have the power to overcome any such offensive, but in the end they find themselves powerless without a team who functions and operates in unity. Both sides need each other in order to find lasting success. The only way we are going to obtain such victory is by putting aside our differences and turning our focus to the real enemy within our stores.

We should look at history and understand that great things can come about when brothers quit fighting against brothers. We have allowed civil war to take place within our stores for far too long. It is only when we put aside our differences and come together that a reconstitution era takes place. It was after the Civil War ended that our country reunited and eventually evolved into one of the greatest nations in the world. If we had never stopped fighting one another, and remained divided, I assure you that neither side would have made the progress that we have since that time. Great things will happen when a store becomes unified.

Through our years of battle within our stores many have suffered and paid the ultimate price. Stores have risen, and fallen, taking with them their defeated owners. Many sales associates have come and left in defeat. A vicious cycle of destruction has left many weary and wounded. Now that a great awakening is taking place within our stores a truce has been called. Both sides look upon each other with regret and remorse as they see the multitudes of wounded warriors that have survived. Our hearts begin to soften and lead our minds in a new direction. It is a direction of unity and resolve to take back what is rightfully ours. No longer do our stores have to suffer anymore. A new day of peace has arrived as we push forth together united as one again.

As we begin to end our battles within our stores it is important to realize that many will be left wounded and in need of assistance. I encourage you all to extend your hand and help up your wounded brothers and sisters. Let humanity take action with compassion and thoughtfulness. Deal with one another gently as you reunite into a force that can not be stopped. Eventually time will heal the wounds left behind in the civil store war. However, let the scars left behind be a constant reminder that we may never forget, and remain united as one team.

I have a message to any of you who find yourself wounded and weary from the war. It is a message of hope, comfort and healing. If you have read this far then I am certain an awakening has begun to take place within your heart. This book is a gift sent to you from above, giving you the ointment and bandages needed to heal your wounds. I am by no means a preacher, but rather a messenger with a divine message to help you find your freedom. I have faced many of the same battles that you have faced. Like you, I have become a warrior who has left the battle-field wounded many times and survived. It is through my many years in the retail business that I have been gifted special wisdom and insight to help lead you to recovery and restoration. This is your defining moment!

Let it be known that this day a message has gone out to the world of retail that a change is coming. Truth is coming as a light to expose the real issues that have remained hidden in darkness for so many years. We have allowed things like greed and selfishness to blind us from seeing our own misery. The world of retail has been lulled into a deep sleep as we were totally unaware of the circumstances that we now find ourselves in. Now that we have awoken we look around and find ourselves lost and wandering about. The sales floor has become a grind and there never seems to be a satisfaction within. Everyone is desperately looking for answers to give them direction to find lasting success. The time has come for many great leaders to arise and lead the way to lasting success with the message of truth.

Many people in the Christian world would call this a revival. That is exactly what it is no matter what you believe in. It is a time to rededicate ourselves to running our stores based on the core principles of trust, honesty and integrity. It is a time to turn from our wayward ways and back to the things that we used to hold so dear. We must build our stores up on the successes of the past and bring to light the things that keep us from obtaining greatness. It is with this knowledge and insight that you will be able to thrive and flourish in the world of retail sales. So sit back and open up your hearts and minds to receive the truth that will lead the way to lasting success.

In order for such an awakening to take place within your stores it must first start within your heart. That is where the root of true and lasting change is started. I am not asking you to change your religion or what you believe in. My goal is not to convert or preach to anyone. It is my goal to impact your life and your store's environment in a positive way leading you with truth to lasting change. What you choose to believe in on a personal level is your own decision and who am I to judge you. When you allow truth to enter your heart it begins to flow throughout your body allowing it to function and live.

I am certain that there are a multitude of future leaders and superstars out there who have not tapped into their full potential. They are like a well-made electrical appliance that has the ability to operate and do great things. However, unless it is plugged into a power source it is totally useless and will not operate. The truths that live within this book are a source of power that when connected within you will lead you to amazing results. When you begin to apply these truths to your stores, sales careers or personal life then things will begin to happen. Until you choose to do so you will always be a fine-tuned machine that remains un-operational.

What you just read above is something that is essential to creating change and it is called knowledge. It is knowledge that is the key to opening our hearts and minds to change. Once someone becomes aware of their current situation and sees themselves in a new light great things are right around the corner. Whatever faith you believe in will tell you that knowledge is a main ingredient for success. Being of the Christian faith it is pointed out numerous times how knowledge leads you to many things. One of my favorite verses in the Bible on knowledge is Hosea 4:6: "My people are destroyed from lack of knowledge." I find this to be a great truth throughout the world today as well as the retail industry

The fact is that there is plenty of knowledge out there today in the world of sales. The problem is that it is the wrong kind of knowledge. In the paragraph above I stated that knowledge is the key to opening our hearts and minds to change. That is a very important idea to grasp and take hold of. If you stop and think for a moment you will see how the knowledge we have been teaching our sales associates has lead us away from the truth. Look at the way we teach them to manipulate our customers into purchasing. There is much training out there that is driven by greed and is designed to squeeze every cent out of our customers.

It has become clear that we have been led astray with the wrong kind of knowledge. Look at the state we currently find ourselves in. Greed has severed the bond of trust between sales associate and customer. We have never been more disconnected from our customers and find ourselves meeting stiff resistance. There are a multitude of owners, managers and sales associates who lead unfulfilling careers full of despair and regret. Many of us no longer enjoy our jobs and are obligated to continue on in our misery because it is all that we know how to do. All this turmoil has been created because we allowed the wrong type of knowledge to infiltrate our industry. It has taken root and grown out of control like a weed choking out the truth and devastating our land.

With this great revelation that you just received comes a responsibility to react and bring about the change which is needed. Each one of you reading to this point has a calling and purpose to spread the truth and lead others to newfound freedoms in life and their careers. You were chosen with a purpose to be a difference maker and set the sales world on fire with truth. Each of you is a spark that will ignite in just the right conditions to burn away the dying weeds of deception and greed. Your newfound passion and energy will be the seeds of truth and fertilizer that will bring about new life into the world of retail sales. Now is your time to take part in your calling for the great awakening. With the power of good knowledge and truth nothing can separate you from your destiny of greatness and unity.

Chapter 5

Beginning the Process of Reconnecting

I am sure by now that a righteous fire has been ignited within, which has you ready to bring truth and newfound freedoms to the sales floor. In order to move forward in implementing change you must first reunite your store and change its environment. It all starts with reconnecting the team as one single unit. Owners and sales associates must put aside their differences and focus on the task at hand for the greater good of the store. By now you have witnessed that many of the things that divide us are petty and meaningless. We have allowed our pride and egos to deceive us and lead us into a meaningless civil war.

The first and most important thing that you must do is surrender. It helps if both sides are willing to surrender but the fact of the matter is – that is not always the case. If you are in a store that is divided and the others have not seen the truth yet it is up to you to surrender. I know it is tough to swallow your pride and admit defeat. That is why the battles have raged on for far too long. Neither side has been willing to back down and start the healing process. Our pride has blinded us from the truth that we each need one another to truly be successful and great.

Even if you feel strongly that you are in the right I ask you to surrender for the greater good of the store. If you continue to be divided you will all lead meaningless careers full of regrets and misery to come. A call for surrender or truce must first take place by communicating clearly and effectively your intentions to surrender. If you are an owner who is tired of the conflict and friction, you can be a leader who calls both parties together to sit down and discuss your differences. If you are a sales associate who feels mistreated or powerless, you can call a private meeting with ownership to discuss your feelings. This is how the process of change will almost always begin when one side puts away their weapons and chooses to quit the fight.

When one side makes a choice to stop the fighting a few things will happen. First the other side will have no opponent to resist them anymore thus taking away the power of their aggression. Many of you may be wondering what if I surrender and they maliciously assault me or wound me when I am unarmed. The fact is that is a possibility, but very unlikely to take place. Why? Because the many witnesses who see your intent on surrendering will keep them from doing you further harm. What would happen in war if one side decided to surrender and the other side was unrelenting and vicious? The international community would not stand for it and would rise up against that country for its crime and injustice.

There may be a case or two where the hurt is so deep that the other side will not stop for any reason. If that is the case than then it may be time to part ways and move on in a different direction in life and your career. If you leave the fight, or its environment, than there is no battle to be fought. However, I believe that there are many cases out there where a simple surrender and an open line of communication will start the process of healing and reconnecting. It is in most people's nature to have compassion and forgiveness when a surrender or truce is called. If your opponent is not willing to sit down and discuss your differences than there is a better environment waiting for you to find.

The second important part of the reconnecting process is found in opening the line of communication. When information begins to flow it brings to light knowledge that may help you resolve your issues. Sometimes it is just as simple as that. However, there are times when the lines of communication can get interrupted frequently by lingering hurts and bad memories. It is important to see and understand this when the communication process is taking place so you will be able to maintain an effective dialogue. How many times in your relationships have you come together with the intention of resolving an issue only to watch it reignite and engulf the whole entire process? If you are not gentle and thoughtful during the communication process this scenario could easily take place.

So at this point you have called a truce or surrendered. You have now come to the table to sit down and discuss your differences with respect, and opened the lines of communication. What do you think must be done next in order to become reconnected and unified? You must work together to meet one another in the middle to where both sides leave feeling good within. This of course is easier said than done. Many people want to take, but are not as receptive to giving in return. In order to find a true middle ground both parties must be willing to listen and react in a way that brings about change. This is often the most difficult part of the process.

There are two main things that stand in the way of you reconnecting and finding success. They are pride and deep-rooted hurts. In order to move forward you must expose these things yourself and manage them throughout the process of peace. Both of these issues that cause division are powerful enemies that work within us to ensure that we remain divided. So how do you overcome these great enemies within? Now you find yourself having a battle within yourself that is hard to fight. Sometimes we are so exhausted from our previous battle that we are too weak to stop our own enemies within. Without the proper knowledge or guidance we often find ourselves unable to forgive and forget and move on to greater things. We have now become our own worst enemy. Wow! What a great truth that is. I hope you are truly listening and soaking in this valuable truth.

The best way to overcome your enemy of pride within is to understand it and how it operates. Pride is one of the most deceptive enemies that you will face in life. Many times it takes root within us without us even having a clue. While we are focused on other issues it sneaks in the back door of your mind when you are not paying attention. It can take good things that occur in your life and use it against you. Take the victory of success as a great example. When you are successful there is a great sense of accomplishment. You are pleased with your efforts and relaxing in the moment of sweet victory. However, it is at this very moment that pride enters and begins to plant seeds of deceit in your mind. You begin to think thoughts like I must be really good. Then it grows to thoughts that I must be better than everyone else. Now you feel entitled to something different than everyone else.

You see pride works together with deceit to give you a false reality of greatness. In the process you are viewed by others as arrogant and very overrated. The funny thing is that you are so blinded by your pride that you do not recognize the errors of your ways. This leads you down another path away from truth and straight to disconnection and distance from those around you. Hopefully you can see just how deceptive pride can be when it operates in your life without your knowledge. It is always important to be on guard and look for the signs of pride operating in your life.

The signs of pride controlling your life are witnessed in many different ways. The first key sign that pride is at work is self-recognition. Have you ever witnessed that coworker who is always patting themselves on the back or pointing out their accomplishments? It can get very irritating very quickly. Instead of waiting for other to acknowledge their achievements they are quick to beat everyone to giving themselves praise. Many times people don't want to be around this type of person. In fact they often find great amusement when that person goes through a time of trial or frustration. They are not so quick to lend a hand and help them out.

The second sign that pride is at work is the feeling of

entitlement. That person feels as if they are better than everyone else and that the rules do not apply to them. We have all fallen into the trap of entitlement at some point and time throughout our careers. We often look back and realize just how stupid we looked to everyone else. When people discover the errors of their ways with entitlement they are very embarrassed by what they see when it is brought to light. Then there are those who just don't get it. They never see the truth and are constantly going through small peaks and deep valleys with no consistency in their careers. This leads to an unfulfilling career in business life.

The third sign of pride at work within you is disillusionment. You become so twisted in your cords of deception that you are not receptive to truth or common sense. Have you ever witnessed someone become so defiant over a silly situation that it almost cost them everything? How many times does a tiny little molehill become a mountain of resistance? They become so blinded in their quest for victory that they lose all common sense along the way. Again this is something that we have all gone through. The story I shared earlier about me being written up unjustifiably over nothing was a great example of how I allowed myself to become disillusioned. I was so focused on proving my point that I was fully entrenched and ready for battle. Eventually I was smart enough to surrender, forgive and forget. Remember this process later on.

The final phase of witnessing pride at work within is defensiveness and defiance. Have you ever tried to tell someone who is full of pride anything constructive or criticizing? If you have you are well aware that a sharp and precise response will be headed your way with negative intentions. I know this because I was defensive much of my life and thought it was insecurity that was causing me constant friction. It turns out that it was good ole pride working within me disguised as many other things. I am very thankful that this insight was given to me to expose my pride and allow me to defeat it.

Looking at all these issues that define the works of pride must make you wonder what it will take to defeat it. The answer is very simple. You must first gain the knowledge and insight to recognize it, which in fact you just have. Then you must humble yourself and put the brakes on your ego. Being humble is easier said than done. It is our nature to seek approval, prove our point and win at all cost. The best way to be humble is to be silent and think before you speak. It is your words which will dictate the direction you choose to go. The person choosing to be prideful will speak before thinking and often. The person choosing to be humble will take a moment and think things through while choosing their words wisely. I must admit this is still an area I am fine-tuning in my life. I can be very passionate about things that I strongly believe in.

Finally you must be able and willing to throw in the towel on circumstances that are not worthy of a confrontation. When a situation arises that you do not agree with you must be willing to think of the ramifications that would follow and ask yourself, "Is it really worth it?" That story I shared earlier where I defended myself and my actions on the way a repair ticket was written up was one where I should have thrown in the towel. Even though I was right, it would have more beneficial for everyone had I simply said OK, no problem. We see again how that scenario was full of miscommunication, pride and conflict.

Now that you see clearly how pride operates we must turn our attention to deep-rooted hurts. This is the second major factor that hinders you from being able to reconnect during the reconstitution era. In our lives we are often hurt by others but very rarely does it have a lasting effect upon us. Moments of hurt come and go, and the lines of communications are mostly left opened and operational. However, there are defining moments of hurt that can take place which leave a lasting sorrow that grows within and leads you to a disconnection with others. It is here that we must focus our attention and bring to light the decay that lasting hurts can cause.

In order to best display the effects of deep-rooted hurts we need not look very far. How about looking at the examples displayed in your relationships or marriages? It is a fact that we sometimes hurt those that we love the most the deepest. Have you ever said something to your loved one that you knew would hurt them deeply? At the moments of conception those words of anger felt so proper and liberating. Yet as the words left your mouth your heart began to sink as you realized what you had just done. Even in your moments of anger you knew within that you had just delivered a very damaging blow with malicious intent. If only you could take back those few seconds and the words that were spoken, but it was too late. The damage had been done.

There are two common responses to such an attack. The first is to fire back with flaming arrows of your own that you know will reach the very core of their existence. You know them well and what will do the same amount of damage that you have just received. Clearly this is the worst case scenario that will quickly close the line of communication and start a battle. This is how so many heated arguments in relationship can quickly turn to violence in many forms. I am not just talking about physical violence. The assault that is targeted for our loved one can leave emotional scars that take a much longer time to heal. Because we can't see them we forget about them and do not address them.

The second common response to a verbal attack is one of surrender and defeat. The blow was so severe that it caused you to quit the fight and walk away. The sad thing is that many times the person throwing the darts does not really mean what they are saying. They simply could not cope with the situation and wanted to end it with what they knew would deliver the most damage. They are using it as manipulation to control a situation, but we all know that will spin a relationship right out of control. Before you know it you are totally disconnected and far away from one another. This is where many people just give up and separate or divorce. The truth is they actually do still have feelings for one another if only they could reconnect. It just seems too hard and impossible to do.

Now let's return back to the focus of your store and its environment. We often allow the same things to take place within our stores. Because we work together 40-plus hours a week we get to know one another pretty well. We know what buttons to push or where they are the weakest. When a disagreement arises we use this knowledge with negative intent to conquer a situation. Managers are the worst manipulators of using this tactic to get the desired result they seek. I should know because I was trained to use it and was very effective before I understood the ramifications. To any former employees reading this book I want to apologize for this. I was not aware of this insight years ago.

When we take the time to examine our actions and the intent they have then we are able to grow and learn. The problem is that many people do not like to examine their true motives and actions. They feel like they are losing control or power by exposing their mistakes and correcting them. This is really good ole fashion fear at work that is keeping you from your freedom. In just about any character flaw or issue you will find fear involved somewhere. In my first book *Modern Day Selling* I used a whole chapter to show sales associates how fear operates and how to overcome it. I highly encourage you to read that chapter in *Modern Day Selling*.

As I close out this chapter, I would like you to stop and think about the confrontations of the past within your store. Examine them with clarity and truth in order to see the real issues that may have not been resolved. Many of the disagreements within my career that I reflected on could have easily been handled in a quick and easy manner. If only both sides were not so entrenched and ready to hold their ground at all cost. With a little thought and understanding these moments did not need to escalate and leave negative lasting results. Hopefully this chapter has given you hope and you now see that there is a way to reconnect your store and create a unified team.

Chapter 6

The Two Become One Again

Now that we have taken the time to learn how to start the reconnection process we must turn our attention to solidifying the reconnection so it remains strong. Many stores have been unable to make it this far because they have not found success in the beginning process of reconnecting. This may be unchartered waters for many of you. For those who have experienced such a reconnection you know how exciting and rewarding it is to see your hard work and dedication pay off. The process was tough in breaking through many barriers to reach one another. Now the time for healing has arrived where you can put aside your differences and focus together on reuniting and becoming strong again.

It just so happens that I had a life experience that took place which sets the tone for such a moment. I was at work one afternoon when I received a missed phone call from my son Austen. The message went as follow, "Dad, I have been in an accident and I am hurt really bad. I need to go to the hospital." Immediately I hung up the phone and tried to call him back. I remember the thought going through my mind was thinking that he had gotten in a car with one of his friends and that they must be in a car wreck. When he did not answer my return call, panic took place, as the worst possible thoughts began to enter my mind.

Within a minute or two he called me back to explain that he had an accident on the basketball court and ripped his nose in two places at the top. My 15 year old son is 6′ 5″ and was dunking the basketball on a chain-link net. The chain came up under and hooked his nose as he was returning to the ground. I was so relieved to know that he was going to be OK. Whenever you have a moment like that everything else in the world just disappears for a moment. When I arrived to pick him up I surveyed the damage and it was pretty severe. I was wondering just how bad of a scar it would leave. Would he be maimed and gnarled for life? Only time would tell.

Fast-forward and we arrive at the urgent care to see the physician to stitch him up. Seven stitches later and we were on our way home. What a day! Later that night I looked at his nose and it looked just like Frankenstein. It actually looked worse than when it was open. "How was this ever going to heal and look alright?" I thought. The doctor gave us specific instructions on how to care for the wound and protect him from having a bad scar. It was to be cleaned often and kept away from water and sunlight. When he was to play basketball he would have to wear a mask to protect it from direct contact. I still regret not taking a picture of him with that mask on. It made him look psycho and intimidating. I encouraged him to snarl at the other team and use it as intimidation. Of course he did not listen to me.

A week later we returned to the doctor to have the stitches removed. I was amazed at how well it had healed in only six days. All my worries and fears were put to rest and the scar was not very noticeable. I could not believe how well the body could heal itself in such a short period of time with the proper stitching and care. I think many of you can see where I am going with this. A wound was created and needed attention. If not properly treated it could cause infection and many other issues that would be lasting. Last chapter was like exposing the wound and beginning to check out the damage. This chapter we move forward into treating the wound and bringing it back to a healthy state.

As I look back upon my son's experience I was able to see a process that needed to take place in order for the healing to begin. It must first be stitched up. As I thought deeper I examined the process thoroughly. First the wound needed to be cleaned and inspected. That was very much like the last chapter. Then the area needed to be numbed in order to proceed with the stitching. That was the most painful part of the process but was very necessary in order to stitch him up. I thought and envisioned what would have happened if they had not numbed the area. Austen would have been in great pain and very defiant. This helped me understand why so many people never resolve and heal their wounds.

They did not take the time to numb the area. They just started stitching away and it did not take long for an outburst to happen and stop the stitching together. What a great revelation that was to me.

So as we move forward in the mending process there are some things that you can do which will numb the situation to make it easier to reunite. The first step is to give a sincere apology for your part in the process. An apology is the best way to numb the situation in order to proceed with the mending process. The problem is that many people allow their egos and pride to interfere with their intent to apologize. There was a key word that I used above that makes a big difference. That word was sincere and it sets the tone for the depth of the apology. I would define a sincere apology as an apology given without the expectation of a return apology. The problem is that many of us give an apology with the expectation of receiving a return apology.

Many times the recipient of a sincere apology is not able to give you a return apology at the moment. First, it is because they may not have the knowledge that you have obtained in resolving conflict. Secondly, their hearts may not be softened enough to give an apology. The longer you allow hurt to have a home within your heart the harder it becomes with bitterness and sorrow. An apology is the beginning process of chipping away the hardness around someone's heart, but you must remember that it is a process and could take time to soften. So remember that when others are weak and unable to forgive you, that you must be strong for the both of you. It is a form of sacrifice that you must give to make a lasting result.

The next step was a word used in the last sentence. It is the word sacrifice. Here is the definition of a sacrifice: "The surrender or destruction of something prized or desirable for the sake of something considered as having a higher or more pressing claim." How beautifully does that illustrate the act of forgiveness and mending wounds? You must make a few sacrifices in order to numb the area that you are repairing. What better sacrifice could you give than putting aside your ego and pride? It is a necessary sacrifice in order to achieve a greater good of reconnecting and uniting.

If you are able to do these two things then you will be able to begin the process of repairing the damage that has been done. What do you think that you could use as a stitch to sew together the open wound? The answer is truth! It is the truth that will be your healing agent used to mend the situation. It may look ugly at the time, and even afterwards, but the truth is a bonding agent that will hold together over time. In a short period of time you will be amazed at the results when you re-examine the wounded area and see the job that truth did holding it together.

Just like stitches there are clear instructions to be given on what to do and not do to get the best results. A few days after my son was stitched up we went to the beach for a day. Can you imagine how hard it was for him not to freely swim around in the beautiful ocean water? It took discipline and constant warnings from us to be careful. We constantly reminded him of the lasting negative effects he could have if he disobeyed the doctor's orders. It was very hard for him to follow the rules in place. He actually went under once and was even thinking about taking off his bandage while he was lying in the sun. Why was it so hard for him to resist these pleasures knowing that the damage could be severe? The answer was it was just too good to pass up. He wanted to live in the moment and the future was far away.

How many times have you begun the healing process of mending a situation only to see is resort back into a big issue? You began with a sincere apology, followed by a sacrifice, and then exposed it with the ugly truth. Then something happened! A situation happened that you just could not resist. An avenue was opened for you to point out their mistakes and you took it. Why couldn't you resist? The results are going to be negative in the healing process and you knew this. However, the temptation of enjoying the pleasure of sticking it to them was just too great and the cycle began again. Too many times we do things to intentionally that hinder the healing process and reopen the wounds of the past. It is a vicious cycle that could be never-ending unless you learn to follow the rules set in place for healing.

While you are beginning the process of reconnecting your store it is very important to hold fast to the truths that you have just received. When the situations arise that can lead you to disconnection make sure that you expose them with the truth in order to have a successful healing process. These pitfalls can be avoided if you see them ahead of time. Bringing unity to the store is a process. It takes both sides working together with the same goal and united focus. In order for a process to be successful there are certain steps that must be followed. If you deviate from the plan for success it can have lasting negative results. As always I like to take life experiences to help illustrate these important concepts so there is clarity in my message.

When I get ready for work in the morning there is a process that I follow which makes me presentable to the world. Before I leave the house I must do certain things to clean myself up. The process begins with brushing my teeth in order to make my breath fresh and suitable to be around. This is followed by a refreshing shave that leaves my face smooth and clean looking. When finished it is into the shower where I shampoo my hair and wash my body with soap. After drying off I comb my hair and style it to my liking. Then finally I put on a suit that is well coordinated with fashion and style. This is the basic process that I take daily to make myself presentable to the world.

Now, take a moment and think would happen if I skipped a single part of the process. If I did not brush my teeth my breath could offend many even if I looked amazing. What if I decided not shave anymore but still followed the rest of the process? I would quickly become gruff and stubbly. Over time my face would be overrun with a wild beard taking over its territory. Everything else would look fine, but missing this one step of the process would definitely stand out and be noticed. I don't even want you to think of the consequences of missing my shower or putting on the wrong clothes. There is no way that I would ever be presentable to the world.

I think you can clearly see that the process must be followed in full in order to achieve success. Any part of the process missed could be devastating. Now that you know this I have one important question to ask. Are you missing any key components to the healing process in your store? If so, that would explain why you never seem to find lasting success in being a unified team. I challenge you to follow the process this book sets in place for you. Make sure that you are doing what is necessary to achieve lasting unity.

Understanding the process of unifying leads you to the next step in reconnecting. It is the importance of re-establishing a common trust. When your store became disconnected it was the bond of trust that was one of the first things to be severed by selfishness and greed. It is when people begin to put their needs first that selfishness takes control of the environment and begins to disconnect. This leads others to feel insignificant, hurt and bitter. Our society today teaches us to forget about others' needs and focus only on what makes us happy. This disillusion has blinded many into meaningless and unfulfilling lives. It also has led many in the retail environment into unproductive careers with no support. When the times get tough there is nobody there willing to lend a hand and give them support.

In order to reconnect you must examine your store, as well as yourself, and expose the work of selfishness that is operating in your store environment. You must find what is keeping you from moving forward in the process of becoming a unified store. I have seen the process of how selfishness and greed can quickly sever the lines of communication and trust that is needed to become a unified store. As you are focusing on re-establishing the bond of trust within your store it is important to understand the deceptive work of selfishness and greed.

At this point you may be asking, "How do I re-establish the bond of trust within my store? It sounds great, but it does not seem possible?" If this is you, I know exactly how you feel. It is like standing at the bottom of Mount Everest and wondering, "How will I ever be able to reach the top of that?" The truth is that it is very challenging and will not be easy. The good news is that there are plenty of people out there who have met the challenge and can testify that it is very possible. Of course there are many who have tried and failed. They just did not have what it took to meet the challenge. At this point in the book you must really look within and ask yourself the tough questions. Am I really willing to do what it takes to achieve this unity? Is it even worth attempting such a feat?

Many have looked at the challenge of climbing Mount Everest and simply quit before they ever began. They allowed fear and doubt to master their minds and deceive them into losing hope. Although they may have a desire to achieve such an accomplishment, fear leaves them paralyzed to follow through with action. If these are the thoughts that went through your mind at any point in this book I ask you to open your hearts and minds to truth. Do not be deceived by fear and doubt and lose your opportunity to find lasting success and greatness. Your store and its environment can unite and become a force that is highly effective and efficient. There is a great victory that awaits you at the top when you have faced the elements and remained brave through the journey.

We have already traveled so far towards our destination. You began the journey the moment you purchased this book and did not even know it. It all started with a desire to better yourself and your store. When you witnessed the value and importance of the message of this book you were already on your way. Along the way you have already overcome obstacles and elements that tried to hold you back and slow you down. You have already opened the lines of communication and begun to make the sacrifices necessary to bring about success. You have been exposed to truth that has given you light and clarity to see your way along the journey. The process thus far has not been as painful or tedious as you had once thought.

So here you are halfway up the mountain with your destination much closer than it was before. The challenge that awaits you of re-establishing the bond of trust is an obstacle that you must take on and overcome. Trust is the bandage that protects the stitching of truth. Without it you will be exposed and vulnerable to negative things. The problem is that many people do not like to trust others. The hurts of the past and negative lessons in life have taught them to be guarded and mistrusting. In fact society itself teaches us to not be trusting because there are those out there who do not have our best interests in mind. If they see an opportunity to steal from you or cheat you they will not hesitate to do so. A few bad apples can ruin the whole bunch. Therefore, we have simply become a society that does not trust many people.

Owners and sales associates, what is holding you back from trusting one another? Do you owners fear the sales associates taking advantage of your kindness or generosity? Sales associates, do you feel vulnerable or insecure knowing that the owner has the power on their side? Why not impact one another in a meaningful way by sacrificing what you already have. Sales associates, you need to be kind and generous to your owners first. Quit your complaining and give them your best effort in everything you do. Then, owners give your sales associates the power to be difference makers and achieve great success. Quit allowing fear to keep you from empowering your people. These are a few examples of sacrifice that will lead you to overcoming your fears and doubts, and re-establishing the bond of trust.

It is when we put aside our difference and open up the lines of communications that the bond of trust begins to form again. This is the place where true healing begins within the store and the two become one again. When you have made it this far it is only a matter of moments before you see the results of your efforts and hard work. True healing has taken place and newness begins.

Chapter 7

For the Greater Good of the Store

At this point of the process of creating the Modern Day Store you have overcome many obstacles to achieve the bond of unity. Owners and sales associates have put aside their differences and joined forces to move forward towards a lasting success. The molehills no longer become mountains and there is a new sense of togetherness. Peace has found its way into your store's environment and given you a new vision of your destiny. This is where the special moments of greatness truly begin. As you move forth together to tackle the issues of your store you lead the charge with this important war cry, "For the greater good of the store!"

When both sides are able to put this thought process in action a new passion and energy erupts and begins to consume the enemies within the store. Suddenly fear, doubt and selfishness have lost their power. No longer are their weapons of deceit, division and blindness useful against you. With the weapons of truth, unity and thoughtfulness leading the way you will begin to devour your enemies and take them captive. Now you are an overwhelming force that can not be moved or stopped. This is where the newfound freedoms that you achieve in victory become the foundation of your future.

What a wonderful vision of victory that was in the previous two paragraphs. This is the future outcome of a unified store. However, at this point you have only united and there is much work to be done. Now is the time to turn your attention to the true issues within your store and come up with a plan of attack. What things are keeping you from success? Could it be a lack of sales training because you forgot to focus on learning while your attention was focused on other things that are now defeated? Have your customers been neglected from the superior service you could have been providing them had you not been focused elsewhere? Finally, has your store become dirty and a mess as it took on the character of the environment you had created?

These are the types of questions that you must ask yourself as you begin to plan your points of attack. I encourage you to have a store meeting and strategize together on the things that you need to focus on. Make a list together of the top ten things that you see a greater potential for success in and prioritize them. Then mobilize your team and attack each one in order and do not stop until it is defeated. Below are some suggestions of a few things that might need your attention. These will be the most common things to focus on.

The first area that I highly suggest you focus on would be your store environment. While you were divided there were plenty of negative things that were allowed to operate within your store's environment. You may have put on a fake smile as your customers entered the store but trust me they were aware of the negativity in your store's environment. They could see it on others' faces who were not serving them and were unaware that they were being noticed. Your customers could feel the tension the moment they opened the door.

Then there were the times that you allowed your friction with others to project onto your customers giving them a negative shopping experience. Do not be fooled, they left your store and shared their negative experience with many others. You may have been unaware that your facial expressions were cold or your voice was harsh an abrupt, but your customers weren't. They picked up on it and were turned off immediately. I have witnessed this firsthand on numerous occasions. An owner or sales associate goes to assist a customer after a confrontation, with the stress still oozing through their body. When they speak to the customer they are totally unaware of how harsh or cold they really sound. They have no idea that they have impacted their customer in a negative way.

Now that you are unified it is important to fill your store environment with enthusiasm, energy and passion. When the customers walk through that door they should feel the urgency in your voice, see the gratitude in your smile and know that you care with kindness of your words. Owners, it all starts at the top and trickles downhill. If you are unable to deliver these things then it is important that you find someone who can. It could be your store manager or an elite sales associate who has the ability to lead others. Your people need a leader of energy, passion and enthusiasm to set the tone for your store environment.

Sadly, there are many times that a sales associate steps up to the challenge without being asked and are stopped from delivering their passion and energy into the store's environment. Many owners and managers are bound by fear that they will lose their power if they allow another to lead. So in their fear they smoother out the fire of passion and energy that is catching on around the store. This is a very troubling thing to witness. Owners, I encourage you to empower your people to utilize their strengths to the fullest potential. If you happen to disagree with their assessments of their strengths talk to them and give them a shot. You might be very surprised with what will happen when you mix focused effort and confidence together.

Let it be known that your store environment is one of the main things that sets the tone for your success or failure. This also falls in line with the cleanliness of your store. How often do we get so focused on other things that we allow our store to become a mess? That is one of the areas which was always a high priority in my old store. We had a weekly cleaning chart that rotated weekly to each associate. It was by far the cleanest store that I have ever been a part of. During our six-month cleaning days we even vacuumed the walls. It was actually a little too obsessive for me but it worked. No matter how bad the energy was our store remained clean, which helped mask some of the negative energy.

At this point I would like you to put down the book for just one moment. Step outside your office or desk and take a good look around your store. Even if your store is somewhat clean I assure you with focus and attention you will be amazed at the potential for greater cleanliness. Take what you find and address it immediately. Sales associates, you can address these things too. You do not have to wait and be told to do something. Take pride in your store and have the initiative to act before you are asked.

Usually the store's organization and cleanliness are one of the first things to go when a negative environment settles in. The displays begin to look a little sloppy, things are not put back in their proper place and people quit caring about the cleanliness of the store. They quickly become a product of their gloomy environment. On the other hand a store that is creating a positive store environment will begin to see positive things like extra effort, attention to detail and teamwork. For those of you who have been in the business a while, you know this to be a great truth. You may have not really thought about it until now but that is exactly the way it works.

The next area I suggest that you focus your attention on is the skill level and training opportunities that your staff needs. Sit down together with each sales associate and honestly assess their ability and potential. When you sit down together just ask them what their thoughts are on their ability and potential. You will be amazed at the honesty and openness that you will find when you allow them to assess themselves. The reason this will happen is because they are aware that the whole meeting is an opportunity to better themselves. You are not there to specifically point out their flaws, belittle them or talk down to them. You are now working together to give them the best available tools to be successful.

During your session you should write down their needs and desires. Then together form a plan to address those needs and fulfill those desires. If you have daily 15 minute meetings incorporate the training they need to help them grow. If the topic is too in depth, then save it for a Saturday morning meeting that is an hour long. One by one you will begin to tackle the weaknesses within your employees and your store will benefit greatly. Many of you may be saying, "I have tried this and it does not work that way." The reason this has not worked in the past was because your store divided. Your sales associates were resistant to anything you had to offer. In their minds the store meetings, trainings and talks were a punishment and task. Now together it is a team-building experience. Did a little light bulb just go on inside your head?

You will be amazed at your staff's willingness to learn when the environment is positive and set to benefit each other. The problem is that many of today's stores did not have an answer to create this environment until today. If you are still skeptical, try this out and be amazed at the results. Many things that you have tried before and which have failed will now become successful. That is the beauty of having a unified store. Every answer of truth to your problems that you find within this book will create a new passion and energy within you to go out and conquer. Can you feel it at this very moment?

Connecting frequently with your sales associates is vital to creating a positive work environment. When you, or your manager, take the time to listen to their needs and support them the bond of unity will strengthen. Keeping this in mind, you must go beyond listening, and address their needs. Now that they are listening you will find great rewards in your efforts to plant and grow new skills. Each time you give them the proper attention it is like watering the seeds and adding good soil. This added to the light of truth that you have found will grow into something beautiful and magnificent. If you do not take the time to nurture and care for your sales associates then the efforts will be fruitless.

The last area that I suggest you address goes out to the sales associates. Remember it is a two-way street of give and take. So far most of the pressure has been put upon the owners and the managers of the store to lead your team forward. Now it is your turn to address the issues that many of you may have. I am pretty sure you can guess where I am going with this. Now that you are unified and reconnected it is highly important that you are subordinate and follow the lead of your commander. At this point they have invested a lot to unify your store and create a better work environment. Because they have done so much for you, it is your obligation and duty to march to the beat of their drum under the flag they hold so high.

Now that you are unified your enemies of pride, resistance and conflict have fled. There is no need for you to linger on the past. Now is the time to open your ears and listen to the orders. Take the vision of truth and see your way forward under the direction of your owner. Be prepared to give your best efforts and fight for a cause that you now believe in. When you hear the battle cry, "For the greater good of the store," charge forward without hesitation knowing that your leaders are behind you following closely with support. This is your defining moment of your sales career! Victory and greatness await you!

If by now you are not excited then I have my work cut out to help you see the truth. Everything that I have suggested in this chapter thus far has been done for the good of the store. These are the kinds of sacrifices that the team must make in order to become a force that is unstoppable and victorious. The vision has been laid out before you with clarity. The truths have created a direction towards true and lasting success. Do not let anything stand in your way to freedom and unity. From this point forward may your thought process be led with the saying, "For the greater good of the store!"

Chapter 8

Creating the Modern Day Store Environment

In the previous chapters I have already given you many tools to help you create a wonderful store environment. By now you should have grasped the great importance and value there is in having a positive store environment. I believe that this is so important that I want to dedicate another chapter just to make sure the message is loud and clear. Some of this may seem repetitive but trust me you need to hear it over and over again. The more you hear it the clearer it becomes. We have discussed in great detail many of the things that create a negative store environment. In this chapter we will discuss the benefits of having an amazing store environment.

I want you to take a moment and think about your store environment. When you examine closely what do you see? Are your people happy? Are you happy? Now I ask you to think about the times that your store environment is electric and filled with energy. There is always one time of year when negativity fades away and is overcome with joy. Of course that time of year is Christmas. Stop and think about the difference that you see from December and January. What a difference a month makes right? Why does this happen? The answer is that it does not have to happen. We allow it to happen.

When the Christmas season arrives we are often thrilled and excited because we know it is show time. The store environment becomes electric and filled with hope and visions of prosperity. No matter how many hours you work you wake up the next day ready to go and make some money. All your hard work throughout the year has led you to the motherload of paydays. It is this passion and energy that fuels us to give a little extra effort, work a little longer hours and work together as a team despite our differences. This is the one time of year that all negativity takes a back seat and the store environment is alive and well.

Fast-forward a month and what does your store environment look like? All of a sudden you are not as quick to get up for that return or exchange. Your customers are no longer viewed as a joy. Instead they have now become a nuisance. You find yourself exhausted and looking for closing time to arrive quickly. What happened to all of the positive energy? Why have you resorted back to your old ways? When is this cycle ever going to stop? The answers you will find within this chapter.

The reason that our stores become alive in December is because the air is filled with hope, joy and unity. When these three things enter the store the negative things of your store must go away for a season. They are powerless to operate in such a happy environment. Every December you are given a little taste of what your store environment should be like every day. We have come to accept the fact that it will go back to the way it was, so we allow it to happen every year. That is why January is one of the toughest months of the year to keep up morale. As things begin to revert back into the norm a frustration and sadness enters the store, as we are powerless to keep the enemies of the past from re-entering our store environment.

The questions I have for you are: "Are you really powerless?" "Does it have to be this way?" The answer to these questions is No! The truth is that you have great power to control your store environment and its destiny. The problem is that many are unaware that they even have such power. This is another great truth that will liberate your store and bring about the success you so desire. In order to help you understand it is important that we dissect the seasons to find the answers.

Let's first start by examining why the Christmas season creates such a positive store environment. We already have diagnosed that it is the benefits of hope, joy and unity in play that bring about such change. Everyone is willing to put aside their differences for a season and work together. Why? Because there is money to be made and the conditions are set for success. Making money is not a bad thing. It is OK to be prosperous and successful. However, when it is your only motivating factor you are setting yourself up for a free fall later on down the line.

If you are being totally honest with yourself many of you are coming to the realization that making money is your motivating factor. The problem is when the money is gone and the conditions are back to normal you lose your motivation quickly. In fact you are even worse than before because you had a taste of success. Now you are depressed. The cloud of gloom and doom set in your store, while you buckle up for another long year ahead full of many obstacles. What if I told you there was a better way? What if I told you that your store could be like Christmas all year long? Would you be interested? Then listen up and hear the truth because it is about to come your way like 95 mph fastball.

The reason that your store is unable to maintain the energy and excitement of Christmas time is that your priorities are often in the wrong order. The fact that money is the major motivator sets you up for failure and an inevitable letdown. Now I am not saying that you should not be interested in making money. Let's be totally honest, making money is great. However, when it is the driving factor to your machine, then failure is bound to come. The reason is that your customers are the fuel that operates this passion and energy when they are there spending their money. When they leave, or are no longer purchasing, you are left without fuel and unable to operate. Do I sense another moment when the little light bulb just went on inside your head?

What do you think will happen if you were to replace the motivation of money with more positive things? How would your store change if the motivating factor was customer service and impacting your customers' lives in a meaningful way? What if your motivating factor was unifying your team and creating a wonderful store environment? Don't you think these things would be more lasting? I can assure you that the money will still be coming in but just in greater stacks and frequency. Why? Because your customers will love to shop with you and know that you truly care about them. Your employees will work for you harder than they ever have because they respect you and feel loved. Your store will be changed forever!

I encourage you to teach your staff the importance of putting their priorities in the proper order. Making money should be farther down the list. We have become so focused on making money that we have limited ourselves to finding success. We have missed out on the opportunity to impact our customers' lives in a meaningful way that leaves a lasting positive impression on them. When we fail to do this there is no reason for them to give us their loyalty or trust. That is why the bond of trust has been severed between sales associates and customers. It is good ole fashion greed at work again. In my first book, *Modern Day Selling*, I spent great lengths in talking about this. I encourage you to explore this deeper.

In order to help you see it more clearly let me share with you some insight into my success. Why do you think my books have found so much success? If money was my main objective it would not have had nearly the impact on people's lives as it does today. My top priority is to share this insight with you to impact your life in a meaningful way. You are now my customer. The message and your personal growth are far more important to me than the money. Could I have charged $29.99 for my last book like many other sales trainers do? Sure I could! However, at $14.95 I understood that it would be more affordable to those who really needed it, the sales associates.

When people read my message of truth it creates a desire within for them to hear my message in person. The standard sales trainer would utilize this opportunity to charge thousands of dollars for in-store training. I choose to do it at roughly half the price because my main goal is to revolutionize the sales floor and its environment. Some speakers show up for one hour and ask for $3,500. I show up for two days at the same price. The second day of training I spend one on one with each sales associate to ensure their needs are being met. Before the training event I try and contact each sales associate individually in order to set the foundation of trust and sincerity. I will continue to do so as long as I am able to. Why? It is because my priorities are in the right place. You are my top priority.

Many business people would look at that and say is he crazy? They think that I am missing the boat on a cash windfall. I am being criticized for caring for my customers too much. The funny thing is that they just don't get it. In my mind success has already found me in the fulfillment that I receive in impacting people's lives. The fact that a lot of money has found me along the way is just a bonus. This is the concept and thought process that each and every one of you should bring into your store. When you conduct your business this way people will respond to you in a positive manner and success upon success will find you. I can feel the heat from the light bulb that just turned on inside your head.

These are the greatest truths that are needed in order to create an amazing store environment. In order to achieve this environment your store must go through the biggest loser campaign. Just like the TV show, *The Biggest Loser*, you must leave your bad habits and surround yourself with what it takes to be successful. If you have ever watched the show it is amazing to watch the transformation that takes place. Even the contestants who lose the contest are winners because of the transformation that took place in their lives. Their lives are forever changed because they were willing to put in the time, energy and effort to make a change. Make no mistake, it was not easy. They spent time away from their families, endured long workouts with trainers, and abstained from bad foods that got them the way they were.

There was a price that they had to be willing to pay to find true and lasting success.

It is a sad fact that many retail stores in today's world have become obese with selfishness, greed and unhealthy habits. Over time they did not realize the lasting effects that these things could have until it was clearly too late. By the time they were morbidly obese they had given up hope and accepted their fate of misery and despair. Today, I am here to share with you that there is hope. Just like the trainers on the show this message will be here to give you the hard truth and push you to new heights. Whenever you feel like giving up just look within the cover of this book for the motivation to keep moving forward. You will find all the answers and motivation to move forward in your store transformation.

The ending of the show is always the most rewarding to watch. It is the revealing process to the family and friends that makes your heart leap with joy. They are all overcome with tears of joy and happiness as a new person steps forth with confidence, freedom and a future filled with unlimited possibilities. We all can't help but feel excited as we have watched them go through such obstacles to reach this newfound success. This can be your store if you are willing to put in the hard work, time and effort necessary to achieve such results. It is now time for an Extreme Store Makeover and it all starts with your store environment.

Now is the time that we must strategize together to bring about a positive store environment. There are many things that you could do to impact the store environment in a positive way. For the sake of time I will share with you my top three ingredients. I call them the three Cs: compliment, care and creator. When you are able to bring these benefits to the store's environment your store will never be the same. Before you know it your store will be unrecognizable to your customers, competition and your family. Your customers will be in shock when they come in expecting the same ole service and are treated to an amazing experience. Your competition will wonder what is going on when people begin to purchase from you instead of them. Finally your family will enjoy the benefits of not having to hear you complain for hours a week when you arrive home.

Let me share with you a little more about the three Cs. I will start with my favorite one which is the compliment. The moment that you decide to start complimenting each other and your customers for their accomplishments beautiful things will begin to happen. Here is a great analogy. Let's say that you buy a new suit or outfit and are excited to wear it. The first time that you go to work there is one of three things that will happen. Someone will notice and compliment you, no one will notice at all, or some idiot will hurt your feelings with a negative comment. When it is noticed and complimented it gives you great joy and excitement. This builds within you a confidence that this outfit was the right choice and is going to be enjoyed. Those who did not notice leave you guessing if it might be the wrong choice. Finally the idiot who criticized you left you no choice but to return it and start the whole process over again.

Of these three options it is clear which is the most beneficial. However, many of us often never say anything at all. We are so focused on ourselves and our own needs that the day goes right on by without a word of confirmation. We did not intend on creating low confidence but our silence left them no choice but to doubt their selection. Then there are those who are just down right mean and nasty. They get a thrill out of pushing people's buttons and do not care about the consequences. Luckily most of us have the desire to create the confidence with the other person. However, many times we fail to notice. I share this story with you for a reason. Always remember that confidence leads you to confidence.

Now let's put this process of complimenting into action in our store environment. Owners, when was the last time that you walked up and complimented your sales associate on a great sales presentation that did not necessarily result in a sale? Sales associates, when was the last time you complimented your owners on giving a great store meeting? The answer is not as often as we should. We might think that way, or feel that way within, but rarely do we express it in the form of a compliment. Therefore it lies hidden in the abyss of your mind never seeing the light of day. Make sure and take the time to compliment one another when it is warranted.

The power of a warranted compliment can bring life to a store environment in a hurry. Besides building confidence it brings about a feeling of joy and accomplishment. This is one of the quickest ways to impact your environment in a positive way. The one thing you must be mindful of is that the compliment must be warranted otherwise it will lose its purpose and meaning. Make sure that you are not complimenting just to be complimenting. Make sure it has a purpose and sincerity to it. When a compliment is delivered properly it brings goodwill to the store's environment. Before you know it things will begin to change.

The next ingredient to impact your store environment in a meaningful way is care. When people begin to truly care about one another and their needs, it begins to flow out like an unending fountain of joy. It does not have to be a huge act of caring or kindness. Sometimes the littlest things can bring about goodwill and change. Here are some examples of situations that could happen in your store where caring can create a stronger team.

Let's say a sales associate has previously had a rough night. Their child was very sick and they got very little sleep and were struggling to make it through the day. They are scheduled to get off at 8 pm but your shift ends at 4 pm. Would you offer to stay and cover their extra four hours without being asked? Owners, would you recognize this opportunity and offer for them to leave early even if it meant that you might have to cover the sales floor yourself? This would be a great opportunity to show how much you care. By putting aside your needs and coming to the aid of a teammate your kindness would show that you care.

How about this common scenario? You witness a coworker handling a tough customer. They are dragging them all over the store and finally they leave. In their adventure they forgot to pick up the catalogs that they were showing to their demanding customer. What would you do? I know what many of us have done. We say, "Hey, Ernie, get over here and clean up your mess!" Instead we could show that we care by picking up the catalogs and taking them to him and saying, "Here you go, I got your back. You handled that tough customer with class. Great job!" Don't you think Ernie would be more open to returning the kindness with the second response? When you begin to show one another that you care with acts of kindness, it begins to multiply and changes your environment quickly.

Finally there is the third C which is the creator. It actually is up to you to create your own environment. What you put into your environment is what you will often get back from others. Think about that negative coworker who always has something unproductive to say. Every time they speak they are spewing negativity into your store environment. They do this because they are hurt, lost and suffering. Often they have no idea at how pathetic they actually sound. What would happen if you began to compliment and care for them? After a while they would have no choice but to stop their negativity or change altogether. You, my friend, have just become a creator. By following the laws of truth you have created a change to the environment that they were affecting in a negative way.

Every single one of us has the power to be a creator. We all hold the power of creating change within our store environment. Even when others have not found the answers to freedom, we can still impact their lives and the store environment. When someone discovers the power they possess in being a creator it is an exciting time to witness. The changes that begin to take place are wonderful to watch and experience. I hope this chapter has given you great insight into the ways of creating a wonderful store environment. Your store can be like the holiday season all year long when you get your priorities in order and implement the three Cs.

In closing I want you to understand that these truths are very liberating and can radically change your store environment. However, unless you implement them and put them into to practice they will only be a vision of greatness. My goal is to see you use these tools and master your environment in a positive way. When you do you will be setting the stage for an amazing show that will take place within your store. You will achieve the gift of a Christmas season environment all year long.

Chapter 9

Maximizing Your Store's Full Potential

Now that the store environment is set to bring about success it is time that we turn our attention to something very important. It is the owner's ability to utilize his or her staff to their fullest potential. I have experienced many retail stores who have employees full of potential but are not being given the proper chance to display their talents. This is an issue that I have seen which has hindered many stores from reaching their full potential. So this chapter we will focus on the reason why we miss the boat, and how to recognize potential within our sales associates.

Recently there was a turn of events that happened in the sports world which captured everyone's attention and created a buzz heard around the world. It was LINSANITY! Even if you were not a basketball fan you were familiar with the term Linsanity. Everyone loved the story of Jeremy Lin who appeared out of nowhere to capture the hearts and minds of fans. He was the perfect picture of the underdog achieving newfound success. So how did this happen? What was it that brought about this newfound success?

It all started with a set of circumstances set in motion that provided the golden opportunity for Jeremy Lin to show his talent to the world. He played for the New York Knicks basketball team and they were predicted to have an amazing season. For some reason the team did not gel as expected. Then throw in a few injuries and the stage for crisis was set. The team had gotten off to one of their worst starts in history and the pressure began to mount on the team and the coach. Out of desperation the coach was forced to try new lineups and methods to try and help his team get back on the right track. This is how the world met Jeremy Lin.

The moment that Jeremy Lin entered the lineup the team began to start winning games. Analysts around the country were suddenly talking about Jeremy Lin. Who was this guy? Where did he come from? You see, Jeremy Lin was nobody special to the basketball community. Many players did not even know his name. Within a matter of days he was now the main focal point of the NBA world. Everyone wanted to know more about Jeremy Lin. As stories began to come out the world took notice of a humble man who put his team first and played basketball the right way. When you added this into his newfound success he became a polarizing figure around the world of sports in general. He then became a role model where parents used his story to teach their kids.

There are a few important things that we should learn and take away from this great story. The first is that Jeremy Lin would have never been known to the world had he not been given a chance to play. If the circumstances had not arisen to give him the opportunity none of us would have even known his name. He would have continued to sit on the bench and watch the better-known players get all the glory. It was his destiny that Jeremy Lin would get his chance to show the world his true potential and talent. Once he got his chance we all know how the story went from there.

Owners, I am here to share with you that there are probably a few Jeremy Lins within your store at this very moment. There are sales associates that are riding the bench in certain areas that could be a game changer for you. I encourage you to explore this opportunity to seek out their potential and utilize it before you hit the crisis mode. Unfortunately, many owners wait until crisis mode hits to begin looking for the answers. Even worse they often pass right over the sales associate who could have the answers to their problems and crisis. The reason that this happens is because they simply never knew the talent and potential was there.

Let me give you a good scenario in order to help you better understand. Let's say that your store manager has decided to leave the company. Now there is a need within the store to find leadership and stability. So what do we often find ourselves doing? We begin to look for that proven all-star performer. It could be someone who is tops in sales within your store or a manager outside of the company with a proven track record. That is about as far as our vision goes into looking for a replacement. Then in desperation we make a quick decision and throw somebody in there and let chips fall where they may.

There are a few pitfalls that I see many store owners fall right into. The first is promoting that top sale performer – who most likely is not qualified to manage – to the management position. Owners often assume that other sales associates will learn from their proven selling skills. The problem is that they are playing their top performer out of position. Could you imagine what would happen if Tom Brady was asked to play defensive line? He would get crushed! It is not the best position for him to find success. Tom Brady is known as an all-world quarterback and to think about putting him elsewhere would be foolish. Yet often we find ourselves making this same mistake and there is a big price that will be paid for such a decision.

The next pitfall I often see is the hiring of someone outside the company who appears to be successful. We base our decision on a few tests, an interview and some references. What we failed to notice was that their success may not have been as clear as we thought. Many times they had a great staff who they inherited at their previous job and it masked their many weaknesses. Other times they just got lucky. They found a store at the right time and did not really do much to bring about success. Their store was going to be successful whoever they put in place. Yet here you are handing over the keys to your well-oiled machine and entrusting them to operate it to it fullest potential.

I have actually witnessed this last scenario take place on a few occasions. It was like giving a person who had their pilot's license the keys to a stealth bomber. The moment they tried to take off they crashed and burned. Why? It was because they had absolutely no idea how to fly such a complex machine. All they were capable of doing was flying their little Cessna. Just because they were a great pilot with a Cessna does not give them the ability to operate your high tech machine.

Earlier I had mentioned that I witnessed such an event and the outcome was devastating to the store and the individual. A store that I worked in had hired a sales manager who was a great guy and had some previous success. He passed every test with flying colors and appeared to be exactly what the owner was looking for. So the decision was made to hire this man as we approached the holiday season. They moved him halfway across the country from his family and thus the journey began. Within a few weeks it was very evident that he was not the sales manager that we were looking for. His sales skills were lacking and his leadership abilities were non-existent. However, he was a very nice guy and knew how to ride others' coattails to success.

Fast-forward two months and he was let go on New Year's Eve. I felt really bad for the guy. He had moved away from his family and sacrificed a great deal through the Holiday Season. However, it was the right call and it needed to be made. You see our store was like that stealth bomber. We had elite sales professionals who could mange themselves as well as help others. The bottom line was that you could have put a monkey in a suit and he would have been successful in our store. However, when someone is put in such an environment who does not qualify it is quickly noticed as their deficiencies and weaknesses are exposed.

I am sure many of you have gone through the experience of making a bad hire. It is something that is inevitable and that we all must go through. However, it is from these negative experiences that we can gain great insight and wisdom to help keep us from repeating the same mistake twice. Often owners just discard the bad employee and move forward, missing a great opportunity to explore and truly understand the negative experience. It sometimes is just easier not to acknowledge a failure and try to ignore it. However, we all know what a big mistake it will be to ignore a great opportunity to gain clarity and wisdom. The situation will repeat itself over and over again, leading you to a vicious cycle of frustration. It is when you take the time to examine the situation and expose the true reason why it was not a success that you will find the truth as well as the answers.

After watching this take place I looked at the situation and noticed something very strange. We actually had four sales associates who were already working there who could have been offered the position. Honestly, three of us would have never accepted such an offer because we were too successful on the sales floor. It would have been a demotion rather than a promotion. However, there was one sales associate who I am certain would have taken the opportunity and done a great job. You see this sales associate was the perfect candidate because she could sell above average, relate to people well and manage just about any situation that came about. To this very day that sales associate has not been given a chance to show what she has got. She is a Jeremy Lin just waiting to be found. I wonder if she will ever get her shot to play and perform.

I encourage you owners to be very careful when hiring positions of leadership and importance. You can get away with hiring a bad sales associate here and there, but a bad hire in management could bring you down in a hurry. Make sure that they qualify for the position and are not a square peg trying to fit in a round hole. Look beyond their ability to sell and focus more on their ability to relate with people and certain situations. That top seller most likely should be left alone unless they are very persistent on becoming a manager. More often than not a great sales associate will fail as a manager. Their greatest skills are designed to make sales for the store. Why would you want to diminish that and run the risk of ruining a perfectly good relationship?

It is a fact that many of today's stores are not utilizing their existing sales associates' full potential. If you are one of the rare few who does then I am certain that your store is very successful year in and year out. What we need to examine closely is the reason why we often miss out on maximizing our opportunities and reaching our full potential. The first reason is very easy to point out and that is we simply do not recognize it. After reading this chapter I encourage you to examine your store closely and take a deep look into each of your sales associates' potential. When you do you will be amazed at the opportunity that you find. Many times it is just that easy and simple.

When you really take the time to see your people with clarity then you will find the knowledge that appears to have been hidden from you. Actually it was right in front of you the whole time, but you just were not looking for it. I have witnessed the most unlikely candidates step up and impact the store in a powerful way. Just like Jeremy Lin they seized their chance and took full advantage of their opportunity.

In *Modern Day Selling* I shared with you the story of Ty. He was a young man who applied for a sales position that I decided to pass on because he did not fit the image that I perceived a sales associate to have. I allowed his long blonde braided ponytail and his rock band past to blind me from seeing his true potential. It turns out that he became the most dynamic sales associate that I have ever witnessed to this very day. He was hired down the mall and began to demolish us instantly with absolutely no retail sales experience at all. There was a steep price that I had to pay for missing that opportunity until he was promoted and left the mall. There is so much more to the story but for the sake not of being repetitive I will move along.

The next reason why sales associates often never reach their full potential is one of the retail store's classic enemies. It is good ole fashioned fear. Many owners and managers allow fear to keep them captive and unable to reach new levels of success. They are simply afraid of losing power and a sense of purpose. They fear that if they allow others to do certain jobs better than they do then they will no longer have a purpose or meaning within the store. This could not be further from the truth and is one of the biggest lies out there. That is why so many of you owners are stressed to the max and carrying such heavy loads that lead you to exhaustion.

If the previous statement really hit home and spoke to you, then I am very happy that you are beginning to see the light. I have seen many owners and people of high positions leave the world of sales behind, bitter, broken and lost. They allowed fear to operate within their decision making and thus control their ultimate destiny. The sad thing was that if they only knew the truth then they could have had a totally different outcome of their career. That is why next chapter we will deal with fear and help you find freedom from its power. I want to make sure that everyone who reads this book has the opportunity to set themselves and their store free from such control. It is my hope and desire that today will be a defining moment in your life and sales retail career.

I think it is very important to point out that there are two types of potential that need to be discussed. There are evident potential as well as hidden potential. The stories of Jeremy Lin and Ty are excellent examples of finding hidden potential. Their stories are unique and special because everyone was unaware of the great potential they possessed. When given a chance they took the opportunity and excelled. Now I want to turn our attention to your sales associates who have the evident potential. These are the sales associates who have displayed glimpses of their potential at times and you know that it exists. For different reasons you have never asked or allowed them to use their special skills. This is where I believe that many retail stores are missing the boat.

After thinking for a moment you may have realized a few of the following scenarios. The new sales associate who is craving new information and is full of passion and energy. They are willing to put in the time and effort to learn and grow, yet nobody is offering them any information. The potential for their success is great, but without the proper information, guidance or time they are left struggling. In the craziness of business life they are quickly forgotten and left behind to fend for themselves. This is where the saying "Only the strong survive" rings very true. Their potential is evident but often wasted.

Let's look at the situation where a store is losing a massive amount of profits in the repair department. The sales associates are not trained well enough to examine the items properly and are missing many needed repairs that are noticed after the fact. Because of their ignorance you are now responsible to fix what they missed. Yet on your staff is a sales associate who always does things the proper way and excels in that area of repair. Did you allow them the chance to share with the staff the secrets to their success? Could they have been used to help train others how to be more efficient and productive? Yes! However, you have never given them an opportunity to use their skills and maximize their full potential. There is that little light bulb again going on inside your head.

Finally, let's examine that sales associate who is not cut out for the sales floor. Even with the proper training they just do not possess the skills set to find success. It is very clear that you need to fire them, right? Wait a minute, there is an opening in your store for an office position. It is very evident that they are well organized, precise and well respected. They are very skilled with using computers and know your system well already. Wouldn't this be a great opportunity to maximize their full potential? Yet many times we often fire them without even thinking it through and are left with two needs. Even worse we sometimes allow them to stay on the sales floor and drag us all down.

These are just a few of the many situations that we see take place within our stores today that could be managed in a different direction. It all starts with a different focus and mindset on looking at each individual's skills sets and measuring their full potential. Only then will you have the opportunity to set into motion a plan of maximizing your store's full potential. Now that the team is unified and moving in the same direction you will be able to lead the way in creating the Modern Day Store.

Chapter 10

Exposing Fear and Finding Freedom

I am sure by now that you have become aware that greatness is right around the corner for your store. The light is getting brighter as you approach the end of a very dark tunnel. As your excitement and enthusiasm begins to grow something begins to happen. The light at the end of the tunnel that was beginning to shine brighter and brighter has suddenly begun to disappear. It is evident that something has stepped in your way, and is trying to block you from reaching your destination of freedom. As it approaches you, it begins to snarl and hiss as its massive footsteps bang into the ground. The closer it gets the darker it becomes around you. Now you are stopped dead in your tracks and are paralyzed from moving forward. It becomes evident that fear has arrived and it is not happy. What are you going to do?

The following analogy is precisely the exact scenario that will take place when you are about to find your way to freedom and newfound success. It is fear who will try and intimidate you from finishing the long journey to freedom. Only when you have the proper courage to face your fears will you be allowed to gain access to your freedom. It is through my experiences with fear in a store environment that I have witnessed the only two outcomes available. You either press forward to complete your successful journey or you fail and are consumed by your fear. The choice is up to you.

There is one important thing that you must know before you face your fears. It is the fact that fear is never as vicious or intimidating as it is perceived to be. That large shadow that is heading your way with intimidating noises is really nothing to fear at all. It is an illusion of power and strength that many are deceived by.

The truth is that fear is powerless once it is exposed with the truth. Many are often amused and relieved when they press forward with courage and find that fear has disappeared. That confrontation that they were expecting was not going to place. The truth is that fear is actually a coward itself when it does not have control over you.

I would like to share with you a few experiences that I have witnessed where fear was able to hinder a store from reaching its destination. The first situation is one where I was involved and it was very sad to witness. As I began to grasp the concepts of Modern Day Selling a few opportunities presented themselves for me to share this insight with my fellow sales associates. I was asked to do 15-minute presentations of my newfound insights during our Saturday morning meetings. As I began to speak and show them these new truths it began to impact the store in many positives ways. My fellow sales associates were beginning to unlock their full potential and the winds of change were blowing fast. Then it happened.

It was during a Saturday morning meeting that I had decided to give them my newest material and really wanted to wow them. I was going to teach them how to overcome their fears and impact their lives in a meaningful way. The session was a huge success! Everyone approached me afterwards asking me for more information. Many wanted copies of my notes. I even had one person approach me in tears, letting me know how this had changed their life and that they were going to use it beyond the sales floor and in their own personal life. The feeling that I got was one of great satisfaction. These were my friends and I was able to impact their lives in a positive way. It was this meeting that opened their eyes to see that Modern Day Selling was going to be big and had true potential to bring change to the sales floor.

Later that day the owner asked me to come upstairs and have a private meeting with him. I was expecting more accolades and a great big pat on the back. What I actually got was a great big slap in the face. The owner proceeded to scold me saying, "How dare you encourage everyone to leave the store!" I did not even see it coming! I could not believe that he interpreted such a wonderful moment in such a negative way. I was stunned and quickly found myself searching for answers. I quickly responded in shock, "What meeting did you attend this morning? I did not encourage anyone to leave the store. In fact I just gave them a great truth that will bring you many new successes." Over time I came to realize that it was actually fear at work within the owner and it was just trying to keep its control.

Later I went to his wife and shared this meeting of confrontation with her. I asked her what she thought about the meeting. She thought it was great and got the same positive energy and excitement that everyone else had. I then asked her how it was possible for someone to come to any other conclusion. Her answer was a valuable teaching moment for me. She replied, "He simply hears what he wants to hear. There is nothing I can do to change his mind. In his mind it is reality." It was then that I realized that not everyone is going to receive my message of hope, freedom and change. I had to prepare myself that others were not always going to agree with me. There was definitely a dark side that existed and would try to oppose such truth at any cost.

The end of the story is that the owner never asked me to speak again at Saturday morning meetings. That was my last training at the store and the momentum quickly shifted back to a negative environment. I was informed to not talk about any of my newfound success while working in the store. So I respected his wishes and continued to work there until I reached a certain level of success where I could leave the sales floor and begin traveling and speaking. I look back upon those four or five meetings that I gave and relived all the positive results it was bringing the store. We were headed towards the next level of success and my coworkers were much happier with their newfound success. I could only imagine where we could have gone if we were allowed to continue the sales training.

This was a classic situation where the owner had the opportunity to utilize some of the freshest insight in the world of sales training. He was not willing to maximize his store's full potential because fear had taken control. This insight had the potential to revolutionize his store and help him achieve a greater success. To everyone who was there it was clear and evident that my message was a powerful truth. The results were amazing, so why would the owner take such offense to positive momentum and success. The answer was that he was allowing his life and career to be ruled by fear. Somewhere along the way fear took root within his mind and like a weed it grew out of control and he found himself entangled in a mess. Over time he lost hope and was left powerless, to follows its illusions and deceptions.

I want to be clear that I still respected and followed the owner's wishes. If you are in a store environment where ownership has not yet found the truth, then it is your duty to respect them while you are working at their store. Who knows, maybe that owner is reading this book right now and a liberating moment is taking place within. My goal is to expose the things that hinder us from reaching new heights of success, and give people the truth that they need to defeat their enemies. That is why I am taking a full chapter to expose the work of fear and show you how it operates within a store environment.

By now I am sure that you can clearly see the ways of fear and how it operates within a store environment. In *Modern Day Selling* I shared with you how fear works together as a team. Fear leads you to doubt, doubt leads you to false reality, false reality leads you to shame and ultimately shame leads you to defeat. It was the owner's fear that lead him to the false reality that everyone would take this truth and better themselves, thus making them want to leave. What a shame it was that the momentum was shifted in a negative way, which led to the defeat of missing four of the next five months' goals by large amounts. Hopefully this scenario will no longer need to take place within your store because now you know the truth and can see it with more clarity.

The next experience where I witnessed fear at work within a store environment was also a very disturbing event to watch unfold. I was unfortunate to witness a mentor and friend fall captive to the power of fear and it almost cost him everything. For the sake of keeping his identity safe we will call him Anakin Skywalker. Anakin entered my life as our store manager who was full of retail life experiences and was confident and very capable of running a store. He was a perfect fit into the dream team that we had already assembled. We accepted him with open arms and he quickly became one of us. Together we found greater success to the tune of a $1,500,000 increase over two and half years. This was all done during tough economic times also. The future looked very bright.

The problem was that there was an evil emperor who was in charge and had other plans for Anakin. Over the two and half years this evil emperor allowed his fear, bitterness and anger to slowly chip away at Anakin's confidence, leading him to doubt his worth and abilities. It was this doubt and false reality that led Anakin down a dark path leading to his demotion and humiliation. Anakin was stripped of his power and another manager was brought to power while he humbly took a back seat in shame. It was this humiliation and shame that led to bitterness and anger of epic proportions to build within him. Before long he was transformed into the same evil that the emperor possessed and thus became Darth Vader.

The person we once knew who possessed confidence and success was no longer in existence. He had changed into the likeness of his master. He became very critical, was always snapping and very unhappy within. Unlike the movie *Star Wars* we were able to free Anakin and help him find his freedom. You see Anakin was the person who approached me in tears and thanked me for sharing with him the insight on how to overcome his fears. He began to quickly change back to his normal self and did not allow the fear of the evil emperor to consume him any more. No longer were the threats, demeaning comments and fear tactics taking their toll on Anakin. He had found the answers to his problems and was able to free himself. Shortly afterwards he left the company and found a better situation, and to this day is successful and happy.

In retrospect I guess the owner was right about his fear of everyone leaving. You see the truth exposed the dark environment that he had created. He knew that once the people began to see the light and find freedom, he would be powerless to control them and keep them under his thumb. Within a few months of that meeting the leadership of the store began to leave and find better jobs elsewhere. They were tired of being abused and unappreciated. Hopefully you can see now why I put so much emphasis on ownership leading the way and creating a positive work environment. If you continue to allow fear to control your decisions then your sales associates will find this newfound success and move forward with or without you.

All it took for Anakin to create true and lasting change was to see the truth and believe it. Once his eyes were opened he realized exactly what had happened and what was taking place. With this understanding he was able to see things clearly and push right past the intimidating illusion that stood in front of him. He was headed to freedom and nothing was going to stand in his way. The fear that consumed and controlled him no longer had its power, and a time of change and newness was forthcoming.

Owners, I am quite sure that many of you do not allow fear to operate within your store to the magnitude that it did in that store. However, I ask you to use this insight and find the areas where fear might be operating within your life and your store. Your fear often takes root and grows in different sections of the store. If it is not exposed and dealt with, it will grow out of control and will consume the whole store. Here are a few examples of areas where fear might be operating within your store.

The first area I will address I spoke of earlier in the book. Fear is often found operating within the balance of power within the store. It is what divides us and keeps us captive. Owners often fear a loss of control and power if they utilize their sales associates' assets and full potential. Sales associates fear a loss of control and dignity if they submit to the owners every wish. When both sides are free of this fear then they are able to operate as a team and move mountains together.

Another area where fear often operates is in the policy and procedure area of the store. Many retail stores allow their policy and procedure manual to be written by fear. I have witnessed it numerous times. Let me explain these situations in more easy terms to help you better understand. An unfortunate situation occurs within your store where there is not a set policy in place. Instead of dealing with the individual and the issue you decide to make a new store policy so this unfortunate situation will never happen again. The problem is that often the new policy is written in fear and it limits your staff's ability to be successful. Now everyone must pay the price for one unfortunate situation.

It is when this situation happens repeatedly that a store and its environment become consumed by fear. I want to be clear that there are rules and guidelines in place to protect the store and its employees. The common rules of good business practice should always be enforced and followed. I am speaking of those policies that were implemented as a reaction to an unfortunate situation. Too many stores have become reactionary in their policy and procedure manuals. Instead of having one set of guidelines that everyone abides by, they are often changing and manipulating their policies out of fear. This creates an issue within the store because there is no stability or trust.

The last area I will share with you where fear often operates is in the repair department. I sit back and look at how many different policies and procedures that I have seen written and changed based on negative situations within the repair department. There are so many things out there that cause issues in the repair department that many of us have become obsessed with protecting ourselves to the point of insanity. It has gotten out of control, and it is time that someone stood up and exposed this fear with truth.

"So what is the truth?" you may be asking. The truth is that there are many things out there that you must be aware of and prepared for. In the jewelry industry it is things like fake stones, chipped stones and con artists who look to take advantage of opportunities. In the auto industry it could be false claims or missed repairs that come back to haunt you. Whatever industry that you are in there are issues that you must be prepared for. I want to point out that there is a big difference between being prepared and living in fear. The problem is that many stores choose to live in fear and it can cause many issues within the store.

Earlier in the book I shared with you a story where I was written up over a repair description that was later found to be well written. It was fear that the owner had instilled in the manager to lead him to the false reality that if I did not put the girdle measurements on the repair ticket, then the owner would be upset and the company could be liable. We were all well trained to look out for the company's best interests and paid great attention to detail when filling out a repair ticket. The problem was that it became so consumed by fear that filling out a repair ticket became a really big hassle. The issues that it caused were far worse than a mistake or two that could or could not happen. Everyone hated taking in repairs, which led to sales associates ignoring customers who came in with jewelry in their hands. It was the go-getters like me who paid the price of taking in repair after repair because nobody wanted to do it.

Hopefully this chapter has given you fresh insight into the ways that fear can operate within your store. Now that you know the truth it is up to you to take this knowledge and address the situations. By sharing this information with a unified store you will find many new successes and freedoms to help you become a Modern Day Store. If anyone reading this found themselves or their stores bound by fear and needs more assistance please e-mail me at brian@moderndayselling.com. I will do my best to assist you in helping you find your freedom.

Chapter 11

Taking on the Two-Headed Monster of Selfishness and Greed

In the world of retail sales today there are many challenges that we face in finding true and lasting success. Last chapter we exposed the way that fear operates within your store and its environment. Many truths were shared with you to conquer and overcome this deceptive enemy within. Now we must turn our attention to an enemy that has decimated many stores. It is the two-headed monster of selfishness and greed. Over time these two powerful enemies have joined together to become one major force of destruction that leaves many stores crippled and powerless to defend themselves.

As I mentioned earlier there was a time when business was conducted on the founding principles of trust, honesty and integrity. It was here that a strong connection of trust and communication was established between sales associate and customer. This created an amazing environment that made the customer feel like they were family and set the foundation for lasting success. As the world evolved, many stresses and demands followed with it. The things that we thought would make our lives easier actually wound up creating the mess we have exposed today. This leads many to wonder how this could happen. Why couldn't we see this happening right before our eyes? Within this chapter you will find many of the answers to your questions.

Make no mistake about it, the two-headed monster of selfishness and greed was the master planner of such discon-nection. As the pressures of business life increased it called out to us with many deceptive words and promises of greatness. With soothing words and empty promises it led us away from the path of truth and into a world of darkness. We became so entranced that we were blinded from seeing the truth and became powerless to act. Thus we entered the era of bad sales tactics that were designed to manipulate and trick our customers into benefiting only us and our needs. No longer was the sale about the customer or meeting their needs. It was a season that we look upon now with disgrace as our eyes are opened and we see things with clarity.

It was during this era of bad sales tactics that many sales associates began to find what appeared to be newfound success. The uneducated customer became prey against such deceptive sales tactics. Because they were so used to trusting the sales associates that they dealt with, there really was not much they could do to resist these bad sales tactics. Customers were like lambs being led to the slaughter. For a season they became victims as we gorged ourselves with wealth and profit at the expense of our customers. It appeared that the sales associate would rule the floor and there was nothing that the customer could do about it.

Then something happened! The customer had an awakening just like you are today. Their eyes were opened to see the truth and a righteous anger was ignited within. No longer were they going to be manipulated and deceived. The times and season of change had arrived and there would be a stiff price that the sales industry would have to pay for their actions. The balance of power began to shift as the customer became more educated and began to resist. Thus greed and selfishness had done their work well. The bond of trust and communication had been severed between sales associate and customer. The cold war had begun!

For many years now we have found ourselves facing stiff resistance from our customers. The times of easy sales had totally disappeared. We began to try and implement new things to combat such resistance. We used misleading sales where we jacked up the price only to give the appearance of a big discount. We created certifications and warranties to try and give our customers comfort and reassurance. Now we see many of the certifications and warranties are misleading, deceptive and of very little use. Everything we have tried has eventually failed because of our selfishness and greed. What had the potential to be good was somehow tainted and twisted by others for their gain and advantage. Many of us followed suit leading us even further away from the truth. Oh how the mighty have fallen!

As I mentioned earlier in this book there is a time and season for everything in business life: A time to be awake and a time to slumber; A time to connect and a time to disconnect; A time to unify and a time to be divided. We have suffered for far too long to continue on such a miserable journey. Now is the time and season for us to see the truth and become awakened within. It is a time for us to truly reconnect with one another as well as our customers. Now is a time for the Modern Day Store to be born and bring life into the retail world once again. It all starts with exposing and overcoming the two-headed monster of selfishness and greed.

So far we have exposed the crafty work of selfishness and greed between the sales associates and customer. Now it is important to turn our attention to its destructive work within our stores. Owners, take a moment and think back to beginning days of your store. See with clarity the process in which your store was slowly divided by selfishness and greed. When you take the time to relive those memories I am pretty sure a righteous fire will ignite within you as you discover the many truths. There was a time where your store was operating the proper way and you were building your business on a solid foundation. At what point did things begin to turn? How come you did not see it happening until now? These answers will be found over the next few pages.

Now is the time to give you fresh insight into the ways that selfishness and greed operate within your stores as well as yourself. I am sure there are many forces at work right now trying to keep you from reading this book. The truths that you will find have the power to set you free and lead you to victory. As always we will start at the beginning. The important thing to realize is that selfishness and greed are one of the most deceptive enemies that you will face. Deception is their main weapon that they use in order to begin their work of destruction.

In order for selfishness and greed to use their weapon of deception they must first create a distraction. Have you ever found yourself trying to deal with an important issue only to find many other issues arise to lead you away from the main problem? Make no mistake about it, those things did not just happen by accident. Before you know it you are so consumed in other things that the main issue was left unresolved and exposed for selfishness and greed to begin working. This is almost always how selfishness and greed gain access to your store.

In order to help you better understand let me give you a few scenarios. Let's say that your store is struggling to make the proper profit margins that you desire. You are conducting your business in the proper manner and everyone is doing their best to try and make sales. This is an area that you know is vital to the store surviving and growing. So you begin to focus on ways of being more profitable while maintaining your ethical standards of conducting business properly. You then decide to hold store meetings to have everyone focus their attention on finding the right answers. As the meeting begins you explain the situation and everyone is focused together. Ideas begin to be presented and things begin to start flowing in a positive direction. Then something happens.

At some point during the conversation someone brings up a different issue that may or may not be relevant to the discussion. Now, everyone shifts their attention to this new issue that has come to light. Often the issue is not a top priority, but nevertheless we take the bait and find ourselves addressing the wrong issue. While discussing that issue another issue arises and the pattern repeats itself. Before you know it you are far away from the important issue and overrun with trivial issues. The meeting ends and you all leave exhausted and unsuccessful. You either totally forgot about the main issue or are just too frustrated to approach it again.

The story does not end here. This is only the beginning of a process that many of us fall victim to. A few weeks go by and things have stayed the same or gotten worse. This leads to many frustrations with no answers. Business life has rolled over you like a giant wave and you are just struggling for survival. So you react out of desperation and cut your employees' commission, or begin to nickel and dime them. In return they begin to feel the pinch and start cheating or stealing from one another. Even worse they could be stealing from you! Selfishness and greed have found success using distraction and deception to totally ravish your store and its environment.

I am sure that you could think of many situations where selfishness and greed have taken root by using distraction and deception. As you explore the history of your store I encourage you to use this truth and insight to see their destructive work with clarity. Once you have vision to see how they operate, selfishness and greed will lose their power and effectiveness within your store.

The next weapon that selfishness and greed use to divide your store is the equivalent to a nuclear bomb. It is the disintegrating power of jealousy. When jealousy takes root within a store it consumes the environment and takes focus away from many good things that are taking place. Selfishness and greed thrive off the aftereffects of jealousy's work. In order to help you better understand I will give you a common scenario that takes place. Generally you find jealousy at work within sales associates, but I have seen owners fall prey to its powers as well.

Let's say that sales have been up for a few months and

everyone is doing well. Everyone is working together and customers are leaving happy. As things begin to become more comfortable you begin to slack and take it easy. However, there is a sales associate who is a hard worker and is always hustling to take care of the customers' needs. They are now finding a much greater success and are far ahead of everyone else who has taken their foot of the gas so to speak. Instead of being happy for them, or motivating yourself to get going again, you begin to resent them. Every opportunity that arises to de-motivate them or cause them to look bad you take full advantage of. You may even try to take half of a sale that they made with false accusations or lying. Yet again selfishness and greed have worked their magic and won another victory.

I know that the scenario which I just gave is very extreme but it can happen if you are not careful and observant of these situations. This may seem absolutely crazy but I have seen owners become jealous of sales associates for making too much money. It makes no sense and the smart owners would realize if their sales associates are making big money then they too are making big money. I have witnessed this twice and have had other elite sales associates share the same story. Jealousy has the power to manipulate and deceive just about anyone if they are not aware or paying attention.

At this point I would like to point out that yet again the negative forces at work within our store seem to operate as a team. Just like fear, jealousy and greed have many friends that contribute to a negative outcome. By exposing their true intentions and understanding the way they operate you gain the vision necessary to see your way to newfound freedoms. Now that you see things for what they are, what are you going to do about it? Just seeing and understanding will only make things worse unless you conquer and defeat your enemy. Now is the time for action!

Overcoming selfishness and greed always starts by exposing

it with the truth. It is the truth that gives you the desire to find freedom. Once desire is stirred within it gives birth to hope. Now that there is desire and hope working together it leads you to unity. Ultimately unity leads you to the reward of peace. It is at this point that wonderful things begin to operate within your store. Things like kindness, thoughtfulness, and teamwork. This is the vision of the Modern Day Store but getting there is easier said than done. As with anything it takes a lot of hard work, dedication and focus to bring about such lasting change. Earlier I used the television show *The Biggest Loser* as an example of the type of work it takes to achieve such success.

Unfortunately, many stores may have the desire to create lasting change but will be unwilling to do what is necessary to find success. They have become too addicted to negative things and find themselves quickly resorting back to their bad habits and old ways. It is my goal to be that voice that pushes you through the tough challenges that are ahead of you. You must never lose sight of the truth that you have found. Through this message will come many who will rise up and lead the way to bringing change to the sales floor. Many will take this vision and build upon it with truth upon truth, setting the foundation for a great future.

Having now heard the message of hope, I encourage you to implement the skills that you have to bring about change. When situations arise begin to see them with clarity and act with wisdom, kindness and thoughtfulness. By now you should clearly see the errors of our ways. Selfishness and greed not only disconnected us from our customers, it disconnected us from one another. So far this book has given you many of the answers to the problems that you find on the sales floor today. This chapter is one that I encourage you to revisit time and time again. When seasons begin to get tough again, hold onto the truth and knowledge that you now possess. It will see you through any trial or temptation that comes your way.

Chapter 12

Are You Ungrateful? Be Thankful for What You Have

This morning I set out early to beat the heat and cut the grass. As I began to start I noticed my neighbor standing at the end of his driveway. I said good morning and asked him how is wife was doing after her surgery that she had earlier that week. With a painful look he replied that she was not doing very well. I dropped what I was doing and walked over with great concern. He proceeded to share with me that somehow she had a massive stroke and was not going to make it. They were going to pull the plug within a day or two. My heart sank as he began to break down and share his thoughts and fears with me.

They were just about to celebrate their 46th wedding anniversary. I told him how special that was as that many people could not make it 46 weeks these days. It brought a brief smile to his face and for a moment time stood still. He then began to wonder out loud, "How could I ever get used to living alone again?" The love of his life was unexpectedly taken from him and there were no answers to be given as to why. The grief consumed him as I put my hand on his shoulder to console him. Now we were both crying as reality set in that a defining moment had just happened. His life would never be the same.

As I was beginning to leave he shared something special with me that led me to discover the chapter that I am writing now. He told me that the one thing he missed the most was the routine phone call that he received daily from his wife where they would just talk about any and everything. If only he could have those days back where the phone calls seemed irritating and unpro-ductive. Now he realized more than ever that those were some of life's most precious gifts. He would forever cherish those many calls and look back with fond memories, but coming to the reality that he would never receive a phone call from her again was just too painful.

It was this experience that led me to realize that we should be thankful for what we have before it is too late. Many times we find ourselves so consumed with focusing on the negatives that we miss out on enjoying the wonderful things that people have to offer us. I began to reflect back on my career in retail and a few experiences stood out to me that I will share with you. These are moments that I learned valuable lessons on appreciating what you have. Some of these moments I was involved in and others I witnessed firsthand. Either way I gained great insight on what to do and what not to do.

I will start by sharing a moment that I was directly involved in. I was managing a store in Jacksonville, Florida, and was finding great success. The previous manager had received a big promotion and he left the store with many great pieces in place to be successful. One of those pieces was an assistant manager who was a master at sales. She possessed many of the skills that many sales associates could only dream of. It became very clear that she was a big part of the store's success. I knew from the start that I needed to win her over and make the transition as painless as possible for her. So for the first year we worked very well together and found continued success. It appeared to be smooth sailing from here on out.

Then something happened! The honeymoon phase was over and we began to see one another in a different light. Instead of focusing on her many strengths, I began to focus on her biggest weakness obsessively. Her biggest weakness was one of my biggest pet peeves. I could not stand it when my sales associates were late. Whenever someone was late it always seemed to set the tone for a stressful day. Therefore it became a top priority of mine to make sure that people were on time and starting the day off right with a positive flow of energy and focus.

The problem with my assistant manager was that she could never be on time. She was not just five minutes late, but was consistently 15 minutes late or longer. No matter how much I discussed the issue, disciplined her or threatened her it was all useless. I am convinced that you could have put a gun upside her head and threatened her life if she was late and she would not have stood a chance of surviving. For some reason she just could never get her act together in the morning no matter how early she started. It drove me crazy. I consulted many wise people on the issue and they were certain that we could straighten her up and get her to comply with following the rule of being on time. None of it did any good.

We became so consumed of breaking her of her bad habit that we made her life miserable to the point of almost firing her. Thank goodness I came to my senses and realized that firing her would not be the best business decision. As I backed off and began to accept that this was just who she was her performance began to pick back up. Her passion and energy returned and began to affect everyone in a positive way. I had allowed her one major flaw to lead me down a path that was not very good for the store. As I was going through this a few people thought that I should fire her. Their thought process was if she could not be on time then we did not need her. I am glad that I did not listen to them.

We went on to work together for another year and times were good. I learned to accept her for her weakness and in return she performed for me like very few sales associates could. With her success came a promotion. She was now going to be a head manager and I was about to find out just how much she meant to the store. After she left there was a noticeable drop off in talent which forced me to be on the sales floor a lot more than I should have been. We survived but my job became a lot more difficult and with that extra focus on sales other things began to slip a little. Things like cleaning and office work took a back seat because sales were the number one focus. So now I had a dirty store that was unorganized and I heard about it every time my boss stopped by to visit. If only I could have my assistant back I would have treated her much differently.

I want to be very clear that I am not condoning bad behavior or justifying it. I am simply giving you the truth that we all have certain areas of lives that are flawed. Many can be fixed or adjusted but sometimes no matter what you do that flaw still remains. Before you let it consume you and you make the same mistake, I ask you to examine the situation closely. Many times you will find that the sales associate has many more positive attributes that will far outweigh that one glaring flaw. If you focus on that flaw too intently you will become hypnotized and at its mercy.

The next life experience that I lived took place during the time I was a million dollar sales associate. The store that I was working at was amazing. It had many wonderful things about it that set it apart as a special place. The one big flaw that it had was its time-off policy. We only received two weeks' sick or vacation total for the whole year. This left us very overworked and often burnt out. To make things even worse the owners very rarely let anyone off while they were traveling. It just so happens that they traveled almost every year the same week that my kids were out of school for spring break.

I had put in a request around October to be off the following March because we had found a great deal on a seven-day cruise for the family. The store manager had told me that he was confident that I could have the time off even though they would be gone. They were still dragging their feet on making a decision and the deal was slipping away. My manager told me to go ahead and book it and things should be fine. The next manager meeting when he approached the subject he was told that I would not be able to go on the trip with my family. When he brought to their attention that the store had plenty of coverage and it would not be a real issue, he was quickly dismissed. The decision was made and the setting was just right for an eruption of epic proportions.

Yet again here was a situation where anyone could argue for either side and make a solid case before any judge. I was so upset that I typed up my resignation and e-mailed it the owners. When my wife found out about it she talked some sense back into me, and I took back my resignation fully expecting to miss my trip. It was a few weeks later that they informed me that I could go on the trip with my family after all. I was in total disbelief. Why would they risk losing a million dollar sales associate over something that was really not a problem to begin with?

I later came to realize that it was a power thing and that the owner actually enjoyed watching people squirm and suffer. Because he never took time off and enjoyed life himself he expected everyone else to do the same. As my new career in sales training began to take off it became clear that I would need more time off if I was going to continue working there. Trade shows were inviting me to be a speaker and stores were hiring me to train their staff. The time of my departure was near and there would be a rude awakening in the future for his behavior.

Even as I am writing this book I am missing a two-week trip to the Grand Canyon with my family because my benefits were being threatened to be taken away. I calmly explained that this would be one of the last family vacations for us because my step-daughter was leaving for college soon. His exact words were, "I don't care about your kids. If you are going to continue perusing this new career you will not be going with them for two weeks." Clearly I did not need the money and the store would have been OK without me for two weeks. However, this time I submitted to his authority because my time had not yet come where I could go out on my own. Like I said earlier, there is a time and a season for everything. There will be a time coming where big success will find me and in my absence the owner will realize just how good he had it. For now I suffer for the greater good of the family. If any of you can relate to the previous story there is one thing I must point out. The store itself was amazing and a lot of my major success was found at this location. Everyone could see clearly where the owner was wrong and unappreciative but what about me? Did I allow this one major flaw to consume me to the point where I lost almost everything? I am confident that I would find success elsewhere but starting over in a new place and having to build a new clientele would be very toilsome and unwarranted. The fact is that I am grateful for my job and I decided not to allow that one glaring flaw to consume me any longer. There were too many other good things that the store provided for me to let it all waste away over this one major flaw.

As you were reading the few previous paragraphs I bet you could feel the anger and bitterness as I wrote of the situation. I made it very evident that the owner was being unreasonable and very unappreciative of my skills and talents that I provided his store. I did this so you the reader could relive those moments of your career where injustice had been done. As you relived those moments I threw you a curve ball and spun it back to the middle of the plate of truth. The truth was that I allowed this one flaw to consume me. I forgot all about the wonderful things I had and was willing to risk it all. Hopefully you now see the story that you were reliving in a different light.

How many times in life have you done something out of anger only to realize that it was a big mistake? You may have been justified in your anger but with your reaction came consequences that affected your life in a negative way. It could be that marriage you walked away from or lost only to find that you regretted losing your spouse. Many times it is too late once you have left. There is no going back because the damage that was done was irreversible. In the end you wished you could go back in time and do it all over again. If you only had another chance things could now be different. The problem is that life does not often give you do-overs. Make sure that you learn from these mistakes and see the truth before it is too late. It will save you a lot of heartache and struggles in the long run.

The final story that I will share with you today was a situation where an owner found out the hard way that he should be appreciative of what he had. When I first started working at the high end jewelry store as a sales associate there was a store manager in place who was amazing. He possessed all the tools that define a great store manager. In all my years in retail he was the most balanced manager I have ever witnessed in action. Usually managers are great in one area like sales and figures, but lacking in other areas like respect and leadership. Somehow he had found a way to be the complete package. One minute you loved him and the next minute you hated him but the respect always remained.

In the two years that I worked with him I witnessed the friction between the store manager and the owner. The store manager had many great ideas that could benefit the store immensely but the owner was simply not willing to relinquish his power to anyone. In the end the store manager always respected his authority and did things the way the owner wanted. Through all this he did not bring the staff into this conflict and was very professional. I, however, could see very clearly what was going on because the owner was constantly complaining to all of us about their issues. This went on for about two years until the store manager had enough. One day he just left and moved far away to Hawaii. We never heard from him again.

Since the time of his departure we have gone through two other managers as well as two different seasons with no manager at all. In all that time the store saw some success and growth, but it has never had the stability and growth that we had while the first store manager was in place. During the different seasons there were times that the owner openly shared that he wished he had the first manager back. He did not realize what he had until he had pushed him too far away. I am certain if the owner could take back all the negative comments and do it all over, that he would have treated the manager differently. Instead the store has had very little stability over the last five years and everyone who has taken that position has not lived up the standard that was set.

Owners, having shared these stories with you I ask now that you examine your store and what you have created. Look deeper into the key pieces and elements of your success and ask yourself the big questions. Am I thankful for what I have? Have I missed the good that people have to offer because I have been consumed by a specific flaw? Am I making the same mistakes that were displayed above? Finally, do I want to expose this now and save myself the heartache that will come later? Sales associates, you must ask yourself these very important questions as well. Bringing these things to light will help you find freedom and understanding.

Hopefully this chapter was very beneficial for any of you who may be going through a tough time in your sales career. When you take the time to examine the situation you will often find that there are many more positive things that you could be focused on. Do not allow the one or two flaws to hinder you from a store, or sales career, of freedom and success. We all have many strengths as well as weaknesses that we can improve upon. However, it is important to remember that sometimes there will be a flaw that simply will not change and it is how we handle it that will make all the difference in the world. I encourage you to be understanding, patient and kind in this matter, and you will find a newfound freedom waiting to be explored.

Chapter 13

The Key Elements of Commitment and Effort

Throughout your life there are a handful of situations that arise where you are willing to make a serious commitment. It is these moments that define who you are and set the course of your life. When you find your mate there comes a time of commitment when you walk down the aisle and unite in marriage. If you decide to have a child there is a long-term commitment that you must make to ensure that your child receives the proper love and care that they need. It is in these exact moments that you often find a unique passion and excitement that leads you to the illusion that everything is going to be perfect.

In the beginning everything is wonderful and new. These are some of the most exciting and memorable moments of your life. It is during these moments of commitment that a short-term transformation takes place and our joy overwhelms us to the point of being naïve. In our minds we have visions of the future the way that we would like it to be. We see a lifetime of happiness and joy ahead in that marriage. We see all the wonderful potential that our child could possess. In our euphoric state we fail to listen to those who have been before us. We just can't fathom how this perfect connection could ever go wrong or face a time of hardship and trial.

It is the couple who have recently been married who wake up from their dream world and realize that there is a stranger living with them. As time moves along they begin to see one another in a new light. Those glaring flaws that went unnoticed seem to always be around now. Before you know it they are both questioning themselves and wondering if they made a huge

105

mistake? So what do they often do? They begin a campaign to try and change the other person and eliminate the things that they do not like. This often leads to a battle of wills that starts a vicious cycle that seems to never end. What once seemed so wonderful has now become their worst nightmare.

Ultimately, one of three things happens: A) They figure it out somehow and learn to accept one another for who they are. B) One person submits and surrenders and then leads a life of unhappiness. C) One person gives up and walks away. Unfortunately many people today choose option B and C. I want to be the first to say that nobody should judge them. Many times they do give it all they have, but not being able to find the truth together leads them to surrendering. I have witnessed divorce firsthand and it is a process that cuts you to the very core. Earlier in the book some of my insight on creating unity came from that negative experience of divorce. I have chosen to take this unfortunate experience and use it to help benefit and assist others who are going through the process of being disconnected. If you know someone who is struggling in their marriage you should have them read this book. The truths that I share apply to all areas of life beyond the sales floor.

The one important thing to point out is that it takes both people being committed and working together with effort to make a marriage successful. If one person chooses not to be committed or make the effort then the marriage is most likely doomed to fail. Now that your store is unified I encourage you to choose option A and figure things out together, and press forward to find your freedom. Do not be deceived that there will not be times of trials or testing as you begin to clean up your store and its environment together. When those times arrive it is important to stay the course and remain committed.

Now we examine the parent who has just had their first child. At the moment of birth a commitment is made to give that child everything they could possibly need at any cost. We all want the best for our children, therefore it is easy to make such a commitment. These days it is much easier to walk away from a marriage, but much tougher to walk away from a child who you have committed to. If someone leaves a marriage we feel sorry for them and wish them well. If someone leaves a child they are looked upon in a negative light and judged as being a coward. There was a time when people used to look at a broken marriage this way also, but times have changed. I hope I never see the day where we as a society accept the decision of a parent walking away from their child.

So now we clearly see that there is a higher level of commitment given when you choose to have a child. It is this level of commitment that you must have when you begin to unify your store and take on the enemies within. Only with such a commitment level will you find the purpose and meaning to press forward until the end. Without this level of commitment is too easy to walk away and look for greener pastures, only to find that there are none as beautiful as what you already had. Do not be deceived into trying anything other than the truth.

Since you are still reading I am going to assume that you have chosen to give a high level of commitment to creating the Modern Day Store. With this great commitment comes a responsibility to give great effort. Without effort a commitment is actually worthless. Could you imagine that parent who committed to their child not giving the effort when the baby woke up crying during the night? What would happen if the child needed a diaper change and the parent was not willing to put forth the effort to do so? Their commitment would be useless without effort to follow through when the times get tough.

It is through these life experiences that you will find many of the answers when it comes to commitment and effort. If you have ever had a good experience in marriage then you can use that as a road map to lead to you the same success. If you have had a negative experience with marriage then you have a great opportunity to learn from this negative experience. It is through the negative experiences in life that you can find great wisdom and insight. The problem is that many people choose not to explore such situations to find the answers because the pain and suffering is too much to bear.

There comes a time in everyone's life where a situation arises when a special commitment and effort is needed to bring about change. It is in these moments where we must be prepared and ready to meet the challenges that await us. You will need intense focus and dedication to see you through the process and lead you to victory. Without intense focus and dedication you will find very little success or accomplishment. I would like to point out that I used the word intense right before the key ingredient of focus. It is important to understand that there must be intensity involved in your focus when you are facing your giants. When you are intensely focused on a situation you often find many great truths and newfound freedoms.

In order to help you better understand, let me share with you some situations that some of you can relate to. Anyone who has quit smoking cigarettes before can tell you that it takes an intense focus and desire to see you through the process of quitting. If you were to take away focus or desire you would find yourself quickly resorting back to the addicting act of smoking cigarettes. You may have the desire to quit smoking but often times you lose focus along the way and find yourself unsuccessful in your attempt to quit. Then there are times that you are focused but find no desire to continue on in your commitment. The two must work together in order to find success.

Earlier in my life I was addicted to cigarettes for seven or eight years of my life. I knew going in that cigarettes were bad for my health and that they had many long-lasting negative effects that go along with them. Being young and naïve I did not think the rules applied to me and I quickly found myself trapped in a web of deception. After a few years I became aware of my deteriorating conditions and found a desire to quit smoking being born within. Through many years of failed attempts to quit I found myself beginning to accept my fate as desire began to slip away into obscurity. It seemed as if I would never be able to quit this habit that had taken hold of me.

Then something happened that evened the playing field and gave me another chance. A situation occurred that gave me the motivation to quit. My ex-wife at the time was having an affair that had come to light. As I tried to hold our marriage together I asked her one important question. I asked her, "What could I change in order to prove my love and commitment to you?" Of course she picked the one thing that bothered her the most. It became clear that my cigarette smoking had to go if we had any chance of surviving. She had witnessed me trying to quit numerous time unsuccessfully, therefore this was the perfect chance to prove my love and commitment to her. This created the intensity in my focus that along with desire would lead me to freedom. Since that day I have remained free from the bondage of cigarettes and smoking.

There were already things in place to find the motivation to quit. Things like my health and family, but for some reason it just was not enough. It took a defining moment in life to occur in order to bring about the intense focus necessary to find my freedom. That is what made this time of change different from the other failed attempts. I always had the desire to quit and even sometimes a focus, but it was the intensity that was missing. When you find intense focus and desire working together there is nothing that can stop you from achieving your goal. In my case I just wish that I did not have to hurt so much in order to gain the intensity needed.

I had conquered my addiction to cigarettes, but my victory was very bittersweet. You see my ex-wife still left me a short while later to continue seeing the doctor she was involved with. This brought about scenario number two which many of you can relate to, and that is obesity. After quitting smoking and going through a divorce I quickly found myself at 227 pounds. I was overweight and feeling the effects of it daily with fatigue and shortness of breath. I found refuge in my son who I had custody of, as well as my job. They were my only saving graces as I treaded through the rough waters of life. I was simply existing and trying to find stability on solid ground as the currents of life were sweeping me away.

Day after day I would do what was necessary to survive and would come home and find myself trying to muster up the strength to get through another day. Then one day out of nowhere I found myself wanting to break the cycle and make a change. Desire was born and there was now hope. I quickly realized that I was not capable of doing it on my own. So I met with my doctor who referred me to a therapist that could help me. Seeking this help was exactly what I needed as I quickly lost 42 pounds over the next six months. People who had not seen me in a while were amazed at the transformation that had taken place. I was a new man full of confidence, and ready to move forward in a new chapter of life.

In story number one we saw that it took a defining moment to create the intensity needed to find freedom. The beautiful thing about story number two is that no such moment was needed to stir desire within. All it took was exposing the situation with truth and finding the proper help necessary to achieve freedom. It was an awakening moment just like you received at the beginning of this book where desire was stirred within and a newfound passion and energy was created. I prefer scenario number two and suggest that you continue to seek the proper help so you will not need a defining moment to set the tone for change.

Now that you are committed and are willing to give great effort, it is essential that you maintain the intense focus and desire necessary to bring about lasting change and freedom. Over time I lost the intense focus and desire to watch my weight and I slowly climbed back up to around the 205 pound range and have been teetering there for years now. I am still much better off than I was before, but things could be better if only I maintained the progress with an intense focus and desire. Writing this book has created a stir of desire within me to refocus my attention on this topic. Maybe next time you see me in person I will be a little slimmer.

As you move forward in the process of creating the Modern Day Store, I encourage you to maintain your intense focus and desire that helps keep you committed to the effort of creating change. Make no mistake about it that there will be bumps in the road that will test your levels of focus and desire to bring about change. If you are not careful you will find yourself drifting backwards into the ways of old. The stresses and demands of life can be overwhelming at times and it is in these moments that you must hold tight to the truths you have found this day. It is these truths that will keep you afloat through the floods of life.

In closing it is important to remember that you as a unified store possess such great power and truth. Following through the process of change with an intense focus and desire will be the fuel to your commitment and effort levels. Make sure that you do not lose sight of this very important truth and allow the enemies within to gain an advantage over you. May you always remember the days of old and the oppression you once felt so it will remind you to stay focused and attentive. Freedom is a beautiful thing and should never been taken for granted once it is achieved.

Chapter 14

Understanding Your Weaknesses

The next step in creating the Modern Day Store is the value of understanding your weaknesses and how to use this knowledge wisely. Many people would read that statement and say that all you have to do is fix the weakness and make it stronger. Am I right? In some cases this might be true but the simple fact of the matter is that every single one us has weaknesses that are a part of us. Some of these weaknesses most likely will never disappear. We are all human and with that come weaknesses. Nobody is perfect or will ever be perfect. For any of you who disagree we will just to agree to disagree on this one. There is nothing that anyone could say that would change this simple truth.

Throughout this book so far I have shown you many instances of weaknesses within myself, my coworkers and my family. It is these weaknesses that have actually made me strong. Please take a moment and let that last statement sink in. In my weaknesses I have become strong! It is through these life experiences that I have found great wisdom and insight which have become the truth of my success. If I had not lived through these experiences I would not have found the answers that I present to you this day. Therefore I have used my weaknesses to be my strength.

It is in this chapter that you will find some of the most profound truths within this book. This great truth and revelation alone will allow you to see your life in a different view. Earlier in the book I spoke about defining moments and how they are like pieces of a puzzle just waiting to be put together to see the big picture. It is your negative experiences and weaknesses that you often ignore, or try and forget about, which keep you from figuring out the mysteries of life. That is why I mentioned just how important it was to examine these defining moments and see your life with clarity. It may not be easy to relive such moments but it is essential to seeing the big picture in your life.

Can you imagine the impact this insight would have on many of the broken marriages? What would happen if a couple were able to see one another in a different light? How would things be different if they could learn to accept one another for who they were? Instead of demeaning and belittling one another's weaknesses they could become unified and conquer life together. Many of us spend way too much time focusing on each other's weaknesses to where we often miss the strengths that we each possess. What we have failed to miss is the great strength that we can find in our weaknesses.

Now let's turn our attention back to your store. Take a moment and think about some weaknesses within each of you that will not be changing anytime soon. What things will you discover that may not be your best attributes? With me I know that I can be very hardheaded or stubborn in certain situations. I also know that I lack patience and tolerance with others from time to time. These are a few of my weaknesses that have plagued me over the years and caused me much discomfort like a thorn in my foot. It is not in my nature to change who I am, therefore I have come to the understanding that this is just who I am. Changing those bad traits could have a negative effect on who I am thus canceling out many of the great strengths I have.

Now that I can see myself with clarity I have been able to find peace and comfort in knowing that I am perfectly made to carry out my destiny in life. So now I ask you to look within yourself and see the undesirable in a new light. Be mindful that I am not excusing negative behavior or addictive patterns. However, your life will begin to make sense when you put the pieces of the puzzle together. For instance, if I never smoked cigarettes, had gone through a divorce or made the many mistakes I had would my testimony hold any power? No! It is through these things

that I found many great truths that are able to help others understand and find freedom.

Everything in my life has happened for a reason. All my
defining moments whether good or bad have taken place so that
I could discover in time the hidden truths within of Modern Day
Selling and the Modern Day Store. I challenge you to see yourself
with the same kind of clarity and understanding. Find the
purpose and meaning of your defining moments and unlock your
hidden potential and destiny. When you do then you will be able
to say that in your weaknesses there is great strength to be found.
It is here that the light bulb goes on in your head and your life
will never be the same.

I have always struggled with the shame and humility of going
through two failed marriages. For years I was blinded by my
hurt, anger and frustration where I placed most of the blame on
my ex-wives for walking away. I was raised that you stick with it
no matter the cost and that failure was not an option. These
failures led me to unwarranted feelings of guilt and shame which
quickly turned into anger and un-forgiveness. Over time I was
able to forgive myself as well as my ex-wives but this did not
remedy the situation completely. It was not until I put the pieces
of the puzzle together and discovered my true purpose and
meaning in life that I came to realize that those moments were
meant to happen.

Without going through those defining moments I would have
never gained the proper insight and understanding in disconnection and division. I was able to use these horrible moments in
life and use them to benefit others and impact their lives in
meaningful ways. This knowledge led me to a peace within that
passes all understanding. No longer do I hold a grudge against
my ex-wives. I wish them well and have been able to see the
things that I could have done differently to bring about unity. I
still struggle sometimes with why it has been so difficult for me
to have a unified marriage. I have come to realize that it is the

thorn in my foot which has a purpose and meaning. My whole life was set in motion so that this day I would be a messenger of truth, hope and freedom.

If you have issues in your past that have held you captive with regret I encourage you to find your freedom this day. Begin to put together the pieces of your life so that you will see with clarity the big picture of your life that was beautifully made. Make sure that you do it before it is too late. Have you ever witnessed someone pass away in bitterness and anger? Whatever had happened in their life was weighing heavily upon them and they were trapped. For some reason they were never able to put together the pieces of the puzzle and everything was in disarray. Without understanding they were left in the dark with no vision and insight to see the big picture of their life. If you have been unfortunate to witness such an event than you know very well the pain that I speak about.

I will share with you my experience of just such a situation. It is the story of my Poppy, who was my mother's father. My Poppy was an amazing man who many would define as a saint. He and my grandmother had three children and during that time a defining moment happened. My grandmother was stricken with a dreadful mental illness. For years she was in and out of mental institutions. This put a great financial strain on their family and Poppy had to work three jobs just to keep afloat. Many people encouraged Poppy to divorce his wife so the state could pay for her hospitalization.

My Poppy was encouraged to just forget about her and focus on the kids. The problem was that my Poppy was dedicated and took his vows seriously. So for years he struggled and toiled keeping the family together and dealing with my grandmother's mental illness. I remember as a child meeting my grandmother for the first time when they let her out of the institution right before she died. The scowl on her face was terrifying and you could feel the meanness flowing through the air around her. As we approached I remembered everyone saying in a calm voice, "Rose, this is your grandson Brian and he is here to visit you." What happened next has stuck with me forever. She glared directly at me with the evilest eyes and began to rant and cuss my way. They quickly removed me from the room and that was the last time that I would ever see my grandmother.

As I grew older I relived that moment and asked myself, "How could Poppy do it?" How was he able to stay married to someone so vile and destructive? The answer was true love and dedication. He had the type of resolve and strength that many could only dream of in today's world. However, his faithfulness led to many hard years of mental abuse from her with unimaginable stress of wondering when she might go off the deep end. This would later catch up to him in life because he was never able to piece together the puzzle of these experiences.

Poppy and I had a special bond that was formed when I was a small child. You see I was his first grandchild who lived close to him. Poppy and my parents would tell me stories of how Poppy would take breaks from his many jobs to come over and take me on walks during the day. During my younger years he was a major influence in my life. I remember spending the night at his house and we would watch World War II black and white shows. He would then share with me his experience during the war and how he had to dig foxholes. It was not until many years later that I discovered that he never spoke to anyone else about the war except for me. When I was nine he paid for me to fly with him to California to visit my uncle, aunt and cousins. Those were special times and special memories.

When I was three we moved away and I was not able to spend as much time with my Poppy. As time went on he continued his lifestyle of constant work even though everyone had moved away. At some point in time he realized that a lot of his life had slipped away and that he was totally disconnected from everyone. So he retired and moved in with us for the remaining years of his life. Being a part of our family was a wonderful experience. He had a routine, and every day he would prepare a big dinner for us all to sit down and enjoy together. Life was no longer cruel or discomforting any longer. That is until the change happened.

After a while we all began to notice a change in Poppy. He began to get easily irritated and was always very grumpy. The last few years of his life he became a bitter man and began to withdraw himself from everyone else. Sadly, he was diagnosed with cancer and lasted only about three months. The last time I saw Poppy was in his final days as I entered the room and what I saw did not resemble the man that I knew. Poppy angrily shouted to get me out of the room. I remembered him saying that he did not want me to remember him like that. He was great man and planted many treasures within me that I discovered over time.

In time I realized that he allowed his rough lifestyle to dominate his life long after my grandmother was gone. In his final years he was filled with regret and remorse as he began to put together the pieces of the puzzle in his life. By the time he could somewhat see the resemblance of the big picture it was too late. He died an angry and bitter man. The main thing he never understood was that his weakness being my grandmother could have been his greatest strength. Living through such chaos and pushing through the trials and tribulations had given him a platform to do great things. He continued to live the life that he once knew even when the chaos was gone. This was the fuel that drove him to grief, remorse and regret. In some ways I am very honored and grateful to share my Poppy's story with the world. Somehow his rough life now serves an even greater meaning and purpose. I am sure he is looking down from above with a great big smile on his face.

Many of you may be reviewing moments of your life in your mind of the times that defined you. As you are beginning to piece the puzzle together I encourage you to hold fast to the truths that you now possess. Do not allow the enemies of fear and regret to operate within and hold you back from unlocking your hidden potential. Understand that everything in your life has happened with a divine purpose and reason and it is up to you figure it out by exposing these moments with truth. Never forget that in your weakest moments in life there is great strength to be found. All you have to do is look intently and focus on the big picture of life.

Chapter 15

Putting It All Together

So here we are at the end of a journey looking back at all that we have learned. Hopefully you have stored the many truths within and will use them to impact people's lives in a meaningful way. Every single truth that you were given this day is like a seed that is being planted within you with the potential to grow into something beautiful. With the proper nourishment and care you will soon discover the miracles of life as you begin to unify your store and impact the environment in a positive way. The proper nourishment and care can be used in the form of selflessness, trust, honesty and integrity. This is the light, water, and fertilizer that will ensure positive growth.

As your store begins to flourish it is very important to beware of weeds setting in throughout the garden you have created. These are things like selfishness, greed, fear and jealousy. If at any point you see such things sprouting up, make sure and take the time to uproot them and cast them away to die. If left unattended they will eventually choke out the good growth that has already been established. You must also protect your investment with proper communication, teamwork and unity. These are the pesticides that will keep away the devastating insects like division, strife and chaos. Take the time to look over this insight repeatedly as you are implementing growth into your store's environment. Allow everyone to see this great potential and give them a chance to step in line and follow your leadership.

As I mentioned earlier, the time has come for the Modern Day Store to be born and established to set the tone for this new era in sales. No longer will the enemies of the ages be able to operate within our stores and effect their environment. We now hold the power of truth within our hearts and minds to become a force that is unstoppable. As the enemies we face see the coming army of a unified store they will know that their time of power has come to and end. The days of discord, bickering and backstabbing are coming to an end. The power of fear, selfishness and greed will be stripped away as we take back what is rightfully ours.

This very moment is the start of a new era that will bring about many great accomplishments and newfound freedoms. Warriors will arise throughout the world as they lead others to this newfound freedom and truth. One by one the world of retail sales will fall in line as these new leaders take charge and form a unified army of soldiers of truth. This very day you have a chance to become such a leader in this movement of change that is going to sweep across the nations. Do not let fear and doubt hold you back from taking back what is rightfully yours. Your store and your life were set apart for this very moment to be a part of something special and great. Now is your defining moment of greatness where you will see the big picture of your life.

As I close this book I want to share with you that you are called to be a messenger in this movement of change. By your actions you will lead the way in sharing this message with those who are ready to find their freedom. The world of business and retail is where the start of something divine and special has been chosen to take place. This newfound freedom will eventually flow over into others areas of life and bring about a newfound peace and unity that has not existed in many years. The world as we know it is ready for a change. The days of chaos, defeat and misery are numbered.

In time people will learn the benefits of reconnecting with themselves as they see the positive changes within you and your store's environment. The deceptive vices that have held us down have now been exposed and an awakening of epic proportions will bring a stirring within that will be unending. The world as we know it will begin to change for the better. A new day has dawned and the light of truth brings hope to the world yet again so we can see its beauty. Make no mistake about it, this book found you for a reason and now is your time to rise and shine for the entire world to see.

**BUSINESS
BOOKS**

Business Books encapsulates the freshest thinkers and the most successful practitioners in the areas of marketing, management, economics, finance and accounting, sustainable and ethical business, heart business, people management, leadership, motivation, biographies, business recovery and development and personal/executive development.